Photograph of architects model   *Anshen and Allen, architects*

BLENDING THE OLD AND THE NEW — The endeavor of The Bank of California . . . is to show respect for our neighbors and the architectural charm and graciousness that has earned for San Francisco such an admirable reputation for beauty . . . the harmonious placement of the old and the new, the yesterday and tomorrow.

CHARLES DE BRETTEVILLE, *President*

400
CALIFORNIA STREET

THE STORY OF

THE BANK OF CALIFORNIA, NATIONAL ASSOCIATION

AND ITS FIRST 100 YEARS

IN THE FINANCIAL DEVELOPMENT

OF THE PACIFIC COAST

By NEILL C. WILSON

SAN FRANCISCO, CALIFORNIA

1964

THE BANK WISHES TO THANK

THE FOLLOWING PERSONS AND INSTITUTIONS

FOR THEIR GENEROUS COOPERATION

IN FURNISHING MATERIAL AND PICTURES

SOCIETY OF CALIFORNIA PIONEERS

MR. WARREN HOWELL, JOHN HOWELL, BOOKS

MR. FRANCIS P. FARQUHAR

CALIFORNIA HISTORICAL SOCIETY

SAN FRANCISCO MARITIME MUSEUM

ROY D. GRAVES

OREGON HISTORICAL SOCIETY

WASHINGTON STATE HISTORICAL SOCIETY

DESIGN AND TYPOGRAPHY BY LAWTON KENNEDY, PRINTER

Lithographed by Hooper Printing & Lithograph Company

PRESIDENTS

The Bank of California, National Association
During its First One Hundred Years

D. O. Mills	1864-'73
	1875-'78
William C. Ralston . . .	1873-'75
William Alvord	1878-'05
Homer S. King	1905-'09
Frank B. Anderson . . .	1909-'25
Charles K. McIntosh . . .	1925-'38
Chairman of the Board .	1938-'48

James J. Hunter	1938-'50
Elliott McAllister	1950-'56
Chairman of the Board .	1956-'63
Edwin E. Adams	1956-'62
Vice Chairman of Board .	1962-'63
Chairman of the Board .	1963
Charles de Bretteville . . .	1962-

DIRECTORS OF THE BANK

D. O. Mills	1864-'84
William C. Ralston	1864-'75
Louis McLane	1864-'68
	1868-'73
J. B. Thomas	1864-'65
William Norris	1864-'65
	1866-'67
	1869-'76
John O. Earl	1864-'76
Thomas Bell	1864-'79
Herman Michels	1864-'65
A. J. Pope	1864-'65
	1867-'69
O. F. Giffin	1864-'66
James Whitney, Jr.	1864-'66
Moses Ellis	1865-'66
Wm. E. Barron	1865-'71
Alvinza Hayward	1865-'74
R. S. Fretz	1865-'66
Nicholas Luning	1866-'75
Drury J. Tallant	1866-'75
Louis Sachs	1866-'75
William Alvord	1868; '71-'04
William Sharon	1873-'85
Thomas H. Selby	1874-'75

George H. Howard	1875-'78
E. J. Baldwin	1875-'79
James R. Keene	1875-'77
Robert F. Morrow	1875-'77
Charles Mayne	1875-'94
H. W. Carpentier	1876-'79
Calvin Paige	1876-'79
Michael Reese	1877-'78
Adam Grant	1877-'78
	1879-'04
C. Adolph Low	1878-'80
Jerome Lincoln	1878-'93
J. C. Wilmerding	1879-'90
T. L. Barker	1879-
H. M. Newhall	1879-'82
George W. Beaver	1879-'80
Theodore LeRoy	1880-'82
Charles Holbrook	1880-
James P. Pierce	1880-'81
Myer Lewis	1880-'00
James Freeborn	1881-'88
Antoine Borel	1882-'88
	1888-'09
Edwin W. Newhall	1882-'88
	1909-'15

HARBOUR and CITY of MONTEREY, California 1842.

The Stage is Set

The war with Mexico had ended with victory for the United States. But as 1848 opened, the spirit of Spain and Mexico still ruled California, from southern border to Golden Gate. A little seaport on San Francisco Bay had a few hundred inhabitants. Cattle hides and miscellaneous foreign coins were the currency. Northward in the "Oregon country" Americans were pioneering the Willamette Valley and investigating Puget Sound. The Mormons had colonized near Great Salt Lake. There were scattered settlements in Texas and the Southwest. The remaining plains, mountains, deserts, forests and grasslands from the Missouri River to the Pacific Ocean largely belonged to the Indians.

Then, on January 24, 1848, nine days before California and the Southwest were ceded to the United States, an American found gold on the South Fork of the American River.

In all history there had been nothing like the Gold Rush that followed, by ship, by horseback, by covered wagon and afoot. In one year, 900 wagons and nearly 40,000 people passed Fort Laramie in Wyoming, headed west.

Harbor and City of Monterey, California, 1842.
Monterey was the Capital of California when the state was under the Spanish flag.

By mid-1849, over 200 square-rigged sailing vessels had come into San Francisco Bay. Soon they reached 700. Some ships became hotels and warehouses. The first steamship arrived in October, '49. 1850 brought 36,000 persons by sea alone. The hamlet on San Francisco Bay was a humming city. Towns of importance were springing up in the interior. By September, 1850, California had become a State.

Four Mississippi River steamboatmen helped direct the portion of the mighty tide of immigration coming via the Isthmus of Panama. These were C. K. Garrison, Charles Morgan, William C. Ralston and Ralph S. Fretz. Reports of a booming California river traffic had reached Garrison in St. Louis, where he was a partner in a firm making steamboat engines and wholesaling river-boat supplies, and an active river-boat captain himself. After looking the Coast over he set up the partnership at the strategic Isthmus with his old river-friend Fretz, selling exchange and operating steamships. Charles Morgan, the first man who'd ever taken a sidewheeler from the Mississippi out into the Gulf and around to Texas, and who eventually built and owned more than a hundred vessels, looked after the New York and New Orleans ends of the partnership. Ralston, youngest of the four and last to join the firm, left New Orleans for the gold fields on the bark *Madonna* on July 3, 1849. Fifteen years later he was to launch in San Francisco the West's first incorporated bank.

The trudge across the Isthmus was made afoot or by mule. This was Panama, at the Pacific end, about 1850. Here steamships for San Francisco were awaited.

Ralston, born on an Ohio farm, had been a Mississippi freight clerk for Captain Fretz. He was blue-eyed, sandy-haired, solid-framed. When he landed at the Isthmus and saw the business opportunities there, he was 23. Fretz remembered him favorably and put him to work. Garrison and Fretz were busy at Aspinwall on the Atlantic side of the Isthmus, running their steamship, passenger, freight and forwarding business. Ralston was placed in charge at Panama on the Pacific side.

A hilly bit of San Francisco in early times.

Young Ralston was a man for any emergency. In 1851 the firm's steamship *New Orleans*, with 200 passengers noisily eager to get onward for the port of gold, found itself without a skipper. Ralston took hold. He'd never handled a steam-powered vessel on even a small ocean, and the Pacific was a large one. Master's papers were not required. He took the steamer to San Francisco in 18 days and he brought it safely back. The firm made him a partner.

Garrison, Fretz & Co.—Morgan and Ralston the "& Co."—underwent a change when Commodore Cornelius Vanderbilt of New York, proprietor of steamships, lifted Garrison from the Isthmus by leverage of a large salary and put him to work overseeing the commodore's interests in San Francisco. Within five months Garrison had also found time to become mayor of the city.

A railroad was being built across Panama that soon would upset the firm's travel and exchange business, so Fretz likewise moved to San Francisco. Morgan remained in New York. Ralston stayed on at Panama to wind up the

In the building on the left, Ralph Fretz and William C. Ralston set up a partnership to handle the business of the two Morgan steamers *Yankee Blade* and *Uncle Sam*. A year and a half later, in 1856, the firm of Garrison, Morgan, Fretz & Ralston entered the local banking business at another location, Clay and Montgomery Streets.

Isthmus business. He arrived at San Francisco on the steamship *Yankee Blade* on August 31, 1854. He was 28 years of age.

With Ralph Fretz, William C. Ralston set up a new partnership, its office "adjoining the Chinese Salesroom on Sacramento Street." Fretz & Ralston handled the California business of two Charles Morgan steamers, the *Yankee Blade*, 2500 tons, and the *Uncle Sam*, 2000 tons. Thirty-two days after Ralston's arrival, the *Yankee Blade* struck a rock in a fog and sank with tragic loss of life.

In spite of many financial failures in 1855, the San Francisco papers of January 1, 1856, announced the entry of Garrison, Morgan, Fretz & Ralston in the local banking business, with quarters on the southwest corner of Clay and Montgomery streets.

The early concerns calling themselves banking houses in San Francisco were primarily exchange dealers. They were individuals or partnerships that held deposits of money and gold dust for their customers, bought and sold

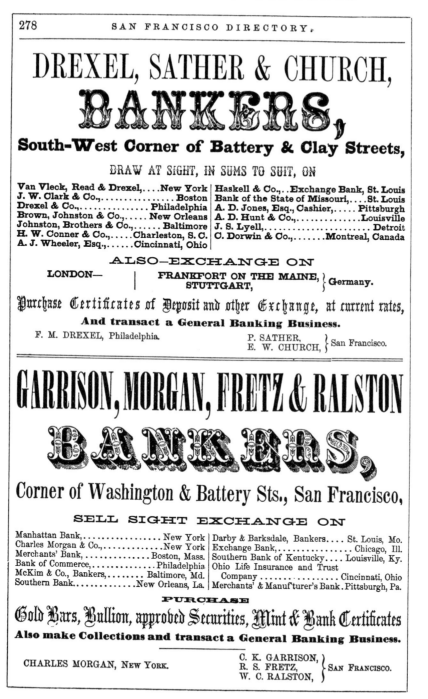

Colville's San Francisco Directory, 1856-57, carried advertisements of Drexel, Sather & Church and Garrison, Morgan, Fretz & Ralston. Both partnerships and also Sather & Church, established 1850, are portions of the "family tree" of The Bank of California.

gold dust and gold bars, loaned funds at high rates, and dealt in exchange drawn on banks, bankers and merchants in other places.

The men of the gold rush brought with them a memory of widespread ruin caused by the collapse of much of America's banking system in the 1830's. It had been an era of highly unsound paper money. At the California convention of 1850, held to write a state constitution, bitter struggle was waged over the phrasing of the article providing for the forming of corporations, especially those that would engage in banking. The law read, as finally adopted: "The legislature shall have no power to pass any act granting any charter for banking purposes; but associations may be formed under general laws, for the deposit of gold and silver, but no such association shall make, issue or put into circulation, any bill, check, ticket, certificate, promissory note, or other paper, or the paper of any bank to circulate as money."

The banking house of Drexel, Sather & Church in the 1850s at northeast corner of Commercial and Montgomery Streets. Founded as Sather & Church in 1850, this in time became San Francisco National Bank and merged in 1910 with The Bank of California.

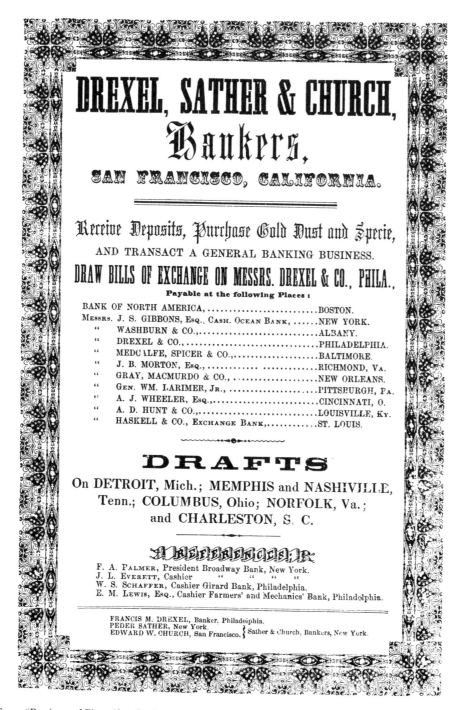

DREXEL, SATHER & CHURCH,
Bankers,
SAN FRANCISCO, CALIFORNIA.

Receive Deposits, Purchase Gold Dust and Specie,

AND TRANSACT A GENERAL BANKING BUSINESS.

DRAW BILLS OF EXCHANGE ON MESSRS. DREXEL & CO., PHILA.,

Payable at the following Places :

BANK OF NORTH AMERICA,............................BOSTON.
MESSRS. J. S. GIBBONS, ESQ., CASH. OCEAN BANK, ...NEW YORK.
   "   WASHBURN & CO.,.................................ALBANY.
   "   DREXEL & CO.,................................PHILADELPHIA.
   "   MEDCALFE, SPICER & CO.,...................BALTIMORE.
   "   J. B. MORTON, ESQ.,........... ....RICHMOND, VA.
   "   GRAY, MACMURDO & CO., ...NEW ORLEANS.
   "   GEN. WM. LARIMER, JR., ...PITTSBURGH, PA.
   "   A. J. WHEELER, ESQ.,........................CINCINNATI, O.
   "   A. D. HUNT & CO.,............................LOUISVILLE, KY.
   "   HASKELL & CO., EXCHANGE BANK,...........ST. LOUIS.

DRAFTS

On DETROIT, Mich.; MEMPHIS and NASHIVILLE,
Tenn.; COLUMBUS, Ohio; NORFOLK, Va.;
and CHARLESTON, S. C.

REFERENCES

F. A. PALMER, President Broadway Bank, New York.
J. L. EVERETT, Cashier   "   "   "   "
W. S. SCHAFFER, Cashier Girard Bank, Philadelphia.
E. M. LEWIS, ESQ., Cashier Farmers' and Mechanics' Bank, Philadelphia.

FRANCIS M. DREXEL, Banker, Philadelphia.
PEDER SATHER, New York.   } Sather & Church, Bankers, New York.
EDWARD W. CHURCH, San Francisco,

From "Register of First-Class Business Houses in San Francisco, 1852." This firm was a predecessor of San Francisco National Bank which was merged with The Bank of California in 1910.

Most of the individuals and partnerships that engaged in early banking in San Francisco soon fell by the wayside, but a few served the public well with their restricted facilities. In D. O. Mills & Company, Bankers, at Sacramento City, in 1849, and in Sather & Church, Parrott & Company, and Garrison, Morgan, Fretz & Ralston at San Francisco, were sown the seeds of what in 1864 became The Bank of California.

Ten months after its start, the banking partnership of Garrison, Morgan, Fretz & Ralston moved to new offices at the southwest corner of Washington and Battery streets. The firm was reorganized following the withdrawal of Garrison and Morgan. Garrison desired to return east, where he went into the railroad business in St. Louis, his old home. Morgan withdrew because his main interest was not banking but ocean transportation.

One of the important customers of Fretz & Ralston was Eugene Kelly & Co., drygoods importers and jobbers. The firm had five partners: Eugene Kelly, Daniel T. Murphy, Joseph A. Donohoe, Adam Grant and Thomas Breeze. Donohoe and Kelly withdrew from the firm in 1860 and it became Murphy, Grant & Co., long a factor in the mercantile life of the West. Donohoe and Kelly had decided to become bankers, joining Fretz & Ralston under a new firm name. On June 1, 1861, the newspapers announced Donohoe, Ralston & Co., bankers.

Kelly went to New York, operating the partnership there under the name of Eugene Kelly & Co. Ralph Fretz remained in the business at San Francisco. Because of advancing years, he asked that his name be no longer used. He became one of the original incorporators of The Bank of California. When he died in 1867, "considering that I have been greatly blessed and that I have an undying attachment to the Government of the United States," he left a bequest of $20,000 to the United States to be applied toward canceling the national debt.

The Bank Takes Outline

The late 1850's were times of action along the Coast, not all of it connected with mining. The first Butterfield overland coach clattered into San Francisco from a 2,730 mile run through the Southwest. Horse-drawn coaches arrived and departed twice a week thereafter, sometimes getting through in 22 days. The Butterfield line lasted three years and was put out of business by the Civil War. The route lay through Confederate territory.

Between Sacramento and Folsom the Coast's first steam train tooted its whistle in '56. The man who'd built that little railroad, Theodore P. Judah, already was dreaming of throwing a line completely across the Sierra and on for the eastern states. The California Steam Navigation Co., organized in '54, had brought most of the steamboats on bay and inland waters under one management.

In Oregon, a group of river skippers was making Portland a key commercial city. In the early '50's, Captain J. C. Ainsworth had taken a sidewheeler from Astoria to Oregon City in 10 hours, and real steamboating had arrived. Ainsworth's associate, Captain Jacob Kamm, built many sternwheelers which were to prove especially adapted to conditions in the Columbia Basin. Soon there were steamboats plying regularly between Astoria and Portland; between Portland and Oregon City; above the Oregon City falls; and up the Columbia to the Cascades. Ainsworth and associates formed the Oregon Steam Navigation Company, set up along the lines of the highly successful California Steam Navigation Company on the Sacramento. The

D. O. Mills
1st President of The Bank of California

WILLIAM C. RALSTON
The Bank of California's first Cashier, 2nd President and the main organizer of the Bank

Oregon company was said to have resulted from a suggestion by W. C. Ralston.

Ralston, optimistic, popular and esteemed, was certain that his adopted city of San Francisco was only at the threshold of cosmopolitan greatness.

CERTIFICATE OF INCORPORATION

The Bank of California was organized "for the purpose of carrying on the banking and exchange business, in all its branches, in this City and within this State, the neighboring State and Territories, and with Mexico; also with the Atlantic cities, Europe, China and the East Indies."

Already the sixteenth city of the nation, San Francisco in his mind would yet challenge Boston's 175,000 Baltimore's 200,000, and New York's three-quarters of a million.

He had brought a comfortable nestegg with him from Panama. He handled his share of Donohoe, Ralston's business with skill. A description of him at this period has come down from one of his intimates, Stephen Franklin, who later became The Bank of California's long-time secretary. "Though somewhat brusque and offhand in manner, he was genial, accessible and winning, of fair presence, manly and magnetic, and of boundless hospitality." Of Ralston the man of vision, another close business associate, Asbury Harpending, later wrote:

For one thing, he had a passionate, almost pathetic love for California. He wanted to see his state and city great, prosperous, progressive, conspicuous throughout the world for enterprise and big things. I think it was his imagination, this ambition, that kept hurrying him into one big undertaking after another, many of which were way ahead of time.*

The famous Pony Express was established in 1860 by Russell, Majors & Waddell, Kansas freighters, to prove that a central route across the continent was the proper place for an overland stagecoach mail. They went broke, but they made their point. The best time they made was 6½ days from the Missouri to a telegraph station just east of the Sierra Nevada. When the ponies themselves had been whipped by the completion of the overland telegraph, letter mail went over the same central overland route by subsidized stagecoaches.

But the West wanted an overland railroad. Congress passed a bill authorizing one, and Judah tried to interest capital. He was turned down by important investors in San Francisco. He then located the support he needed among Sacramento businessmen. Ralston, the man whose vision was as large as Stanford, Crocker, Huntington and Hopkins', saw the rare prestige of the undertaking slip from San Francisco hands, and, after the formation of The Bank of California in the following year, found ample ways to aid the railroad's owners in their unfinished task.

Civil war struck. California lined up for the Union. But when Congress authorized a loan of $250 million and issuance of $50 million in paper money, followed within three months by another loan and $35 million more in greenbacks, the West clung to gold. Greenbacks were accepted only at a discount.

The partnership of Donohoe, Ralston & Company prospered with the rise in the price of gold, as measured in greenbacks. Immense bullion shipments from the mines passed through its hands.

Ralston didn't find it easy to carry all his partners along with him in his view of the Coast's potential. Eugene Kelly in New York raised serious

*W. C. Ralston has been the subject of several interesting books, including Lyman's "Ralston's Ring"; Dana's "The Man Who Built San Francisco"; Tilton's "William Chapman Ralston, Courageous Builder."

THE BANK OF CALIFORNIA.

INCORPORATED UNDER THE LAWS OF THE STATE.

Capital Stock, (*Paid up in Gold Coin,*) $2,000,000.

WITH THE PRIVILEGE OF INCREASING TO

$5,000,000.

STOCKHOLDERS.

SAN FRANCISCO.

D. O. MILLS,	THOS. BELL,	HERMAN MICHELS,	A. B. McCREARY,
WM. C. RALSTON,	JNO. O. EARL,	FREDERICK BILLINGS,	R. M. JESSUP,
R. S. FRETZ,	WM. NORRIS,	GEORGE H. HOWARD,	SAMUEL KNIGHT,
J. B. THOMAS,	J. WHITNEY, JR.,	H. F. TESCHEMACHER,	A. C. HENRY,
LOUIS McLANE,	O. F. GIFFIN,	A. HAYWARD,	J. C. WILMERDING,
ASA T. LAWTON,	A. J. POPE,	MOSES ELLIS,	WM. ALVORD.
WM. E. BARRON,			

PORTLAND, OREGON.
JACOB KAMM.

D. O. MILLS, President.   WM. C. RALSTON, Cashier.

Correspondents in New York, LEES & WALLER, No. 33 Pine Street.

in London, BANK OF LONDON.

The undersigned give notice that the above named corporation has been organized for the purpose of carrying on the Banking and Exchange Business, in all its branches, in this City and with the interior of this State, the neighboring State and Territories, and with Mexico; also with the Atlantic Cities, Europe, China, and the East Indies; for which they are provided with ample facilities, and in conformity with articles of association will commence operations on the 5th day of July next, at the Banking House now occupied by DONOHOE, RALSTON & Co., Corner of Washington and Battery Streets.

With the view of giving to the business of the corporation all the efficiency and promptitude of a private banking firm, together with that confidential seclusion of private business matters so generally desired, the immediate management of its affairs is committed exclusively to D. O. MILLS and WM. C. RALSTON, as President and Cashier respectively, to whom, or either of them, the customers of the Bank will apply in all business matters. The regular meetings of the Board of Trustees will take place monthly.

The undersigned deem it advisable to call particular attention to the following peculiarities of their organization, which are positively binding on all its members:

First.—Sales of its Capital Stock can be effected only after due appraisement by Stockholders selected for that special purpose; and the Trustees of the corporation have, in all cases, the right to become purchasers of the Stock appraised at the appraisement, for the benefit of the remaining Stockholders. This restriction is printed upon each Certificate of Stock.

Second.—Loans cannot be made to Stockholders, except upon collaterals other than their Shares in the Capital Stock of this Bank.

D. O. MILLS,	HERMAN MICHELS,	A. J. POPE,	
LOUIS McLANE,	W. C. RALSTON,	O. F. GIFFIN,	TRUSTEES.
WM. NORRIS,	J. B. THOMAS,	JAS. WHITNEY, JR.	
JNO. O. EARL,	THOS. BELL,		

SAN FRANCISCO, June, 18th, 1864.

The Bank announces its organization. It is the first corporation chartered in California to do a commercial banking business. Later, upon organization of a Clearing House Association, it became *number one*, and retains that number today.

objections to the loan to Ainsworth and other Portlanders to develop their steamboat line. "If you are going to lend money outside California that way, we had better dissolve partnership," Kelly is reported to have said.

Ralston was not impressed by this opinion. What the Coast should have, he was convinced, was a bank attuned to all the region west of the Rocky Mountains, and with resources sufficient to meet western needs.

California's placers, or surface mines, had faltered in the 1850's. But as the Poker Flats and Roaring Camps of the Mother Lode faded, discovery vaulted the Sierra wall.

The overland travelers of '49 and '50, as they approached the Sierra Nevada from the east, had found the way impeded by the sage-covered Washoe Mountains. These were crossed and left behind as quickly as possible. But a few prospectors stayed in the Washoes. Among them were Hosea and Ethan Allen Grosh. They found, in '53, a peculiar muck. "A dark gray mass," they wrote home to Pennsylvania. "Resembles thin sheet-lead." They had found a rich compound of silver. But Hosea struck himself with a pick and died of blood poisoning, and Ethan Allen perished in a blizzard. The other miners in the vicinity did not recognize the black stuff for silver, and went on panning in the gulches for days' wages in gold.

This was the situation until June of '59. Among the gold panners were Pete O'Riley and Pat McLaughlin. They wandered a short way north from Gold Hill, a shack and tent camp close to the overland trail, and dug at the head of a ravine. "They were becoming discouraged," recorded Dan de Quille of the Virginia City *Enterprise* in later years, "but concluded to work where they were for a few days longer . . . and at a depth of four feet, struck into . . . the now famous Comstock Silver Lode." It was gold, however, that had caught their attention.

H. T. P. "Old Pancake" Comstock, a ragtag character, made his appearance on the scene. Continues de Quille:

"Old Pancake had strolled northward up the mountain, toward evening, in search of a mustang pony. He had found his pony, had mounted him, and with his long legs dragging the tops of the sagebrush, came riding up. When the gold caught his eye, he was off the back of his pony in an instant. He elected himself superintendent" and, says the historian, "soon came to be considered not only the discoverer but the father of the lode." In the excitement of the moment, one friend of the miners, known as "Old Virginia" Finney, alias Fennimore, fell and broke his whiskey bottle, but pounded the ground happily and shouted, "I christen this camp Virginia!" So was born Virginia City.

A bit of the muck and ore reached an assayer in Grass Valley. They yielded at the rate of several thousand dollars per ton in gold and silver. All miners in the Washoes were astonished and not a little excited when it was made known that the black-looking muck which miners considered worthless, and were throwing away, was almost a solid mass of silver.

A shaft was sunk on the site of the discovery mine. Its four-foot quartz ledge widened to twenty. To thirty. This was the top of the Ophir mine, which in the next 12 years would disgorge tens of millions. It soon had many companion mines. Two years later, Nevada was a State. Virginia City and Gold Hill, one continuous town, was a place with two populations day and night—one above ground, one below.

In the beginning days, no one knew how to deal with the tough quartz rock below the sulphide-of-silver muck. Here was no strike which a miner could handle with pick and pan. There was much experimenting. Mills would have to be erected to crush the material. That called for capital. Capital was at the Bay. The relation between San Francisco and Virginia City immediately became, and remained, very close.

What was happening in those drab hills east of the Sierra Nevada, '59 to '64, undoubtedly hastened the organization of The Bank of California, colored its early policies, and dictated its size.

A banking statute was enacted in California in 1862, permitting the incorporation of savings banks, joint-stock and mutual. But the need of the times was also for commercial banks, incorporated in order to attract more capital than individuals or partnerships could command. Ralston was sure that this need soon would be recognized.

When the legislature should act, he would be ready. He built his stock subscription list with care. Leading it was the most highly regarded banker on the Coast—head of the oldest existing bank west of the Rockies, D. O. Mills of Sacramento. Twenty-four of the other subscribers were key San Francisco figures in commerce and industry, and one was a Portlander, Jacob Kamm the steamboat builder. Ralston had known him on the Mississippi and the bond was strong.

With a small schooner-load of goods and about $40 in cash, Darius Ogden Mills had arrived in Sacramento in '49. He had been born 24 years before in New York State and had clerked in a store and been cashier of a Buffalo bank. Two brothers had preceded him to Sacramento and were already set up as merchants. Darius Mills preferred the counting-house. "D. O. Mills & Company, Bankers," soon was listed in the directory, at 55 J Street, between Second and Third. When the Sacramento and American rivers went on rampage, Mills' bank along with other business often was flooded. Mills opened a branch at Columbia, Tuolumne County. It is a place sometimes identified with Bret Harte's romantic "Roaring Camp." The brick building which the bank of D. O. Mills & Company occupied took in more than $55 million in gold dust during the branch's existence. In those days Mills, though prematurely bald, wore a drooping black mustache. He was a believer in the stiff collar, the "boiled" shirt and the batwing tie. A contemporary, Mark Hopkins, has said of him that he made every loan with a strong sense of worry about getting his money back. His judgment and integrity were respected everywhere.

Decades later, control of the bank of D. O. Mills & Co. at Sacramento passed to The Bank of California. It was later sold, and the purchasing bank went out of business in the 1930's.

The proposed new bank Mills and Ralston were organizing in San Francisco in the 1860's was quite unrivaled on the Coast with respect to capital and resources. The capital stock, $2,000,000, would be paid up in gold.

On June 13, 1864, its Certificate of Incorporation was filed in the county clerk's office in San Francisco. It was the first joint-stock corporation in the state empowered to do commercial banking. It was organized "for the purpose of carrying on the banking and exchange business, in all its branches, in this City and within this State, the neighboring State and Territories, and with Mexico; also with the Atlantic cities, Europe, China and the East Indies."

A bank, in the 1860's and for many a day to come, was not a place where shoppers dropped in before drifting on to the supermarket. The wage earner and small salaried man at that time made no use of bank checks, but settled his accounts in cash. The new bank was designed to serve business houses and individual businessmen in their financial and commercial undertakings.

Mercantile affairs in California still were very lively and fluctuating. There were probably no people in the world who, in proportion to their numbers, imported so largely of sea-borne goods or who paid such high prices for them. Men made money rapidly and spent it freely. The gold coined at the little San Francisco Mint clinked with a pleasing sound and flew swiftly from hand to hand. Most businessmen were still young, still under the influence of the spell of '49. Boldness ruled.

Cordwood and freight for the mines and Virginia City. Train crossing great trestle over the works of the Crown Point Mine at Gold Hill, 1877. Engines "Truckee" and "Tahoe" double-heading.

The Bank of California Opens

San Francisco, on a Tuesday in July, eagerly grasped its newspapers. The news from the Army of the Potomac was disheartening: Grant was suffering heavy losses at Cold Harbor and the rebels behind Richmond and Petersburg's defenses were defiant as ever. The relentless Confederate raider *Alabama* had caught and burned the Northern bark *Tycoon*, which had sailed from New York for San Francisco the previous March.

Local news was more inspiriting. There had been a town-wide celebration of the Fourth, with parades, exercises, oratory and poetry, and a glittering display of fireworks. The river steamer *Chrysopolis* had beaten the *Washoe* down from Sacramento by fifteen minutes. Maguire's Academy of Music advertised a monster concert of Italian numbers.

Just above Maguire's ad was a modest announcement one column wide by one and a half inches high: "The Bank of California, corner of Washington and Battery Streets, will receive Deposits, attend to the Collection of Paper and draw exchange by Telegraph or otherwise on New York, London, Dublin, etc., on the most favorable terms. D. O. Mills, President. Wm. C. Ralston, Cashier. San Francisco, July 5, 1864."

At the moment the new bank occupied the Fretz & Ralston quarters. The space was probably quite cramped for the 16-man clerical force.

"Steamer Day" was the twice-monthly date for paying all bills and debts and sending remittances to the Atlantic seaboard. Second building on left is the home of The Bank of California, as indicated by the sign. Cartoon by Edward Jump, 1866.

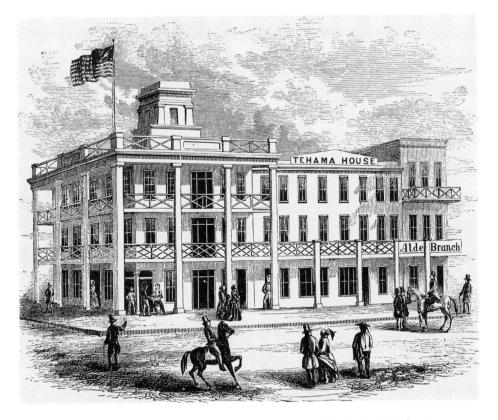

Tehama House, famous early-day hotel that preceded The Bank of California
400 California Street.

Records Zoeth S. Eldredge,* himself a banker looking back fifty years later, "To none but those of the older generation of Californians is it given to know and understand the commanding position held and influence possessed by this great bank. As Minerva sprang full armed from the head of Jove, so The Bank of California came into existence full grown and equipped and was a power from the moment of its birth. . . . The greater mercantile, manufacturing, and business houses at once enrolled themselves among its patrons and supporters and it was with pride that men spoke of their connection with The Bank of California. Its board of directors was composed of the heads of the largest houses in San Francisco; the oldest and strongest banker on the coast was its president and its cashier was considered a marvel of ability, and the ablest financier in California. . . . The best of tellers, accountants, exchange experts, and clerks were employed at high salaries. It was an honor to occupy a position in The Bank of California."

Monetary sums mentioned in connection with the early bank—capital, de-

*Bancroft's History of California, Vol. 5.

posits and the like—do not seem overwhelming to the reader a century later. Many an independent "country" bank has assets as great today as did the nation's giants of 100 years ago. But in 1864, a million dollars was an enormous sum. In that year, more than $2 million was the capital of only two of New York City's 55 banks—the Bank of New York, $3 million; Bank of Manhattan, $2.05 million. They had been in business since 1784 and 1799.

The new bank, its capital all paid up, opened with 506 deposit accounts, showing an aggregate credit of $1,641,605.83; with bills receivable amounting to $1,362,457.05; cash on hand in gold and silver coin and bullion $1,339,061.86; and balances due by correspondents abroad (through Ralston & Fretz), $482,618.84. The "trustees," or directors, held a meeting the following evening. Messrs. W. C. Ralston, Louis McLane, William Norris, J. Whitney, Jr., Thomas Bell, Herman Michels, John O. Earl and O. F. Giffin were present. Stephen Franklin opened the brand new leather-bound minute book and inscribed in the firm hand that would not make a blot or error for the next twenty-five years, "First Meeting—Minutes—Banking House—Wednesday Evening, July 6th, 1864—Mr. Ralston in the chair. On motion it was Resolved that the Articles of

First Head Office (right) completed in 1867 and razed in 1906 prior to the quake. This building occupied the site of the present Head Office, 400 California Street, San Francisco.

Association, Certificate of Incorporation, and the By-Laws, be placed upon the Minutes of the Board, and that the latter are hereby formally adopted."

Immediately the bank set out upon a career of upbuilding the Coast. Stalwart, gracious D. O. Mills was the president, but Ralston of the ranging imagination and vital personality was of equal authority and was chief executive officer in fact and by every act. There were no vice presidents.

Eight days after the new bank's opening, the usual excitement of a Pacific Mail steamship departure enlivened San Francisco's waterfront. The side-wheeler *St. Louis*, Captain Hudson, was leaving at 9 A.M. from the Folsom Street wharf with 262 passengers and $1,896,704 in treasure. Passengers, treasure and general cargo would trans-ship at Panama and cross the Isthmus by rail, and a steamship on the Atlantic side would carry all onward to New York.

The Pacific Mailer's treasure coffers carried the first shipment of gold and silver by The Bank of California. The new bank's portion of the total shipment was $263,166, which was much the largest share.

Ten days after, on July 23, the *Constitution* sailed with $2,158,000, of which The Bank of California's share, $647,672, was four times larger than any other shipper's. The bank's agents along the Atlantic and its correspondents throughout the world were of the finest standing, cemented to the new institution by bonds of personal acquaintanceship with its principals.

The advertisements of the bank from 1864 to 1875 emphasized these connections—"Agents in New York, Messrs. Lees and Waller; in Boston, Tremont National Bank; in London, Oriental Banking Corporation"; and "Letters of Credit Issued, Available for the purchase of merchandise throughout the United States, Europe, India, China, Japan and Australia"; "Exchanges for Sale on the Atlantic cities, drawn on London, Dublin, Paris, St. Petersburg, Hamburg, Bremen, Vienna, Leipsic, Sydney, Melbourne, Yokohama, Shanghai, Hong Kong, Frankfort on the Main."

The Oriental Banking Corporation in London was one of Britain's largest joint stock banks. The Tremont National Bank in Boston had been founded in the same year as The Bank of California, and also with $2 million paid-up capital. Lees & Waller, private bankers in New York, were old friends of Ralston from '49 days when they were commission merchants; in 1866 the firm became Laidlaw & Company. It is still one of the bank's principal correspondents.

Many of the large eastern banks did not operate their own foreign departments, but were content to leave that technical business to the New York branches of European banking houses. But San Francisco of the gold rush era had literally sprung from the sea, a cosmopolitan city of many races and languages brought into existence almost overnight. From the beginning, it had been forced to develop ways of its own to finance the movement of funds and goods to and from distant places, whether the Atlantic Coast of the United

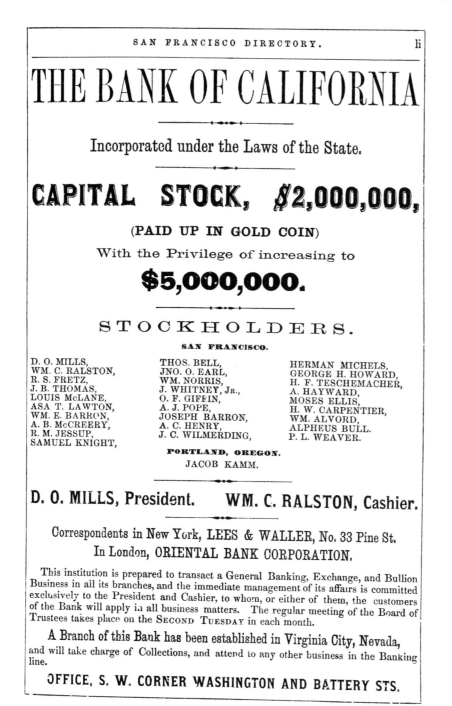

THE BANK OF CALIFORNIA

Incorporated under the Laws of the State.

CAPITAL STOCK, $2,000,000,

(PAID UP IN GOLD COIN)

With the Privilege of increasing to

$5,000,000.

STOCKHOLDERS.

SAN FRANCISCO.

D. O. MILLS,	THOS. BELL,	HERMAN MICHELS,
WM. C. RALSTON,	JNO. O. EARL,	GEORGE H. HOWARD,
R. S. FRETZ,	WM. NORRIS,	H. F. TESCHEMACHER,
J. B. THOMAS,	J. WHITNEY, Jr.,	A. HAYWARD,
LOUIS McLANE,	O. F. GIFFIN,	MOSES ELLIS,
ASA T. LAWTON,	A. J. POPE,	H. W. CARPENTIER,
WM. E. BARRON,	JOSEPH BARRON,	WM. ALVORD,
A. B. McCREERY,	A. C. HENRY,	ALPHEUS BULL.
R. M. JESSUP,	J. C. WILMERDING,	P. L. WEAVER.
SAMUEL KNIGHT,		

PORTLAND, OREGON.
JACOB KAMM.

D. O. MILLS, President.   WM. C. RALSTON, Cashier.

Correspondents in New York, LEES & WALLER, No. 33 Pine St.
In London, ORIENTAL BANK CORPORATION.

This institution is prepared to transact a General Banking, Exchange, and Bullion Business in all its branches, and the immediate management of its affairs is committed exclusively to the President and Cashier, to whom, or either of them, the customers of the Bank will apply in all business matters. The regular meeting of the Board of Trustees takes place on the SECOND TUESDAY in each month.

A Branch of this Bank has been established in Virginia City, Nevada, and will take charge of Collections, and attend to any other business in the Banking line.

OFFICE, S. W. CORNER WASHINGTON AND BATTERY STS.

The Bank's advertisement in the San Francisco Directory of 1865, shows it still at Washington and Battery Streets, and with a branch open for business in Virginia City, Nevada.

The business office of The Bank of California, corner of California and Sansome Streets, in the 70's.
From a sketch by Walter Yeager.

States, Europe, mid-sea islands or Asia. In pre-railroad days, freight and money forwarding even with the eastern seaboard was handled as "Foreign."

From the day it opened, the bank was thoroughly successful. At the meeting of the shareholders of May 5, 1866, it was voted to increase the capital stock to $5 million. During the first two years the bank earned a million dollars, paid dividends of one percent per month, and accumulated a large surplus.

Fitting quarters for the rapidly growing bank were needed. For some years the city's business district had been moving southward along Kearny, Montgomery and Sansome streets. One substantial building, the Merchants Exchange, had been put up on California Street east of Montgomery. On the opposite side, at the northwest corner of California and Sansome, was a property that had been a lumber yard in '49, and was currently occupied by the Tehama House, formerly Jones' Hotel. Its corridors had been brightened by the uniforms of dashing army officers. The future General Sherman had lodged there. Captain U. S. Grant had come down from his post at Trinidad in Humboldt County, and sat on its steps smoking his pipe in contented unawareness of the vast command soon to be his. Ralston had taken his bride there after a honeymoon in Yosemite Valley.

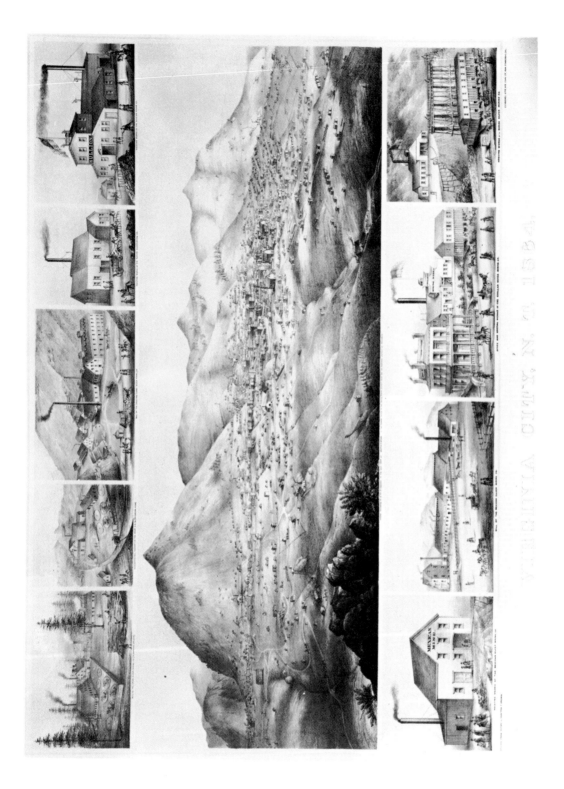

VIRGINIA CITY, N. T., 1864.

In wide California Street, the bank's management perceived an artery of the future. Purchase of the Tehama House land, 67 feet 6 inches on California by 80 feet on Sansome, an area much less than that of the present banking premises, was authorized on December 13, 1864, for $67,500. The frame hotel was moved on rollers to Broadway below Kearny, where it carried on in reduced glory as the Rock House until the fire of '06.

Architects designed a solid structure of two stories, with arched windows flanked by stone columns, the whole surmounted by a stone balustrade topped with ornamental vases. For its place and time, the building was an impressive one. Its cost was about $250,000. The exterior walls were of a hard bluish stone quarried from Angel Island in the Bay. The main entrance was on California Street. There was a bullion entrance around the corner on Sansome. The *Daily Alta California* for June 17, 1867, reported: "The removal from Washington and Battery Streets . . . was made yesterday and last night, and a right lively time the clerks and attaches had in transferring their books and papers."

The banking room occupied the entire ground floor. The original arrangement had wide mahogany counters without grilles, wickets or cages. Gold and silver coins were stacked beside the paying and receiving tellers. Double eagles were piled in stacks of twenty, or $400 per stack. By the use of scoops, any desired number of stacks could be lifted from the trays with no lost motion. Gas lamps with green glass shades stood at intervals along the counter and glowed warmly on dark days. The ledgers were huge leather-bound volumes.

William C. Ralston occupied an inner glass office in the banking room. He was readily accessible. Stephen Franklin, secretary of the bank, sat nearby in flaring collar and black silk stock. His ivory-headed cane was hooked to his desk.

Thomas Brown was assistant cashier. Dour and difficult and of iron rectitude, he was useful counterbalance to Ralston's open hand and heart. Ralston saw that money was lent and Thomas Brown saw that it was paid back.

Women employees were non-existent in that ornate banking room.

The Bank and the Comstock

Five years after the Comstock Lode's discovery, Virginia City had a population of 5,000. Twenty-one miles of shafts and drifts had been excavated and over 60 mills were working on the Washoe County ores.

Ralston had been interested in the Comstock mines since 1860. Upon incorporation of the Ophir Gold & Silver Mining Company in that year, he was made its treasurer. When Gould & Curry was incorporated, followed by Savage, he became treasurer of those companies as well. By '64 he was treasurer of most of the important Comstock mines.

A decline in Comstock fortunes came with exhaustion of the black sulphurets near the surface. The underlying quartz ores were not yet recognized. When the important Gould & Curry mine tobogganed from $6000 a foot of frontage down to $700, its over-extended holders were obliged to let go. Their principal creditor was The Bank of California, to which they owed $40,000. William Sharon, at San Francisco, had applied to the bank for a job. Ralston sent him to

Concord stagecoaches and the stagecoach robber both appeared in California in the later 1850's. The first railroad, Sacramento to Folsom, began operating at about the same time.

WM. SHARON

The power behind The Bank of California's Nevada operations

Virginia City to make an investigation. Born in Ohio as was Ralston, and five years the elder, Sharon had arrived in California with the '49 migration. He had operated a store in Sacramento, then was a partner in a San Francisco stock brokerage firm that failed.

Going over the Comstock ground very thoroughly, Sharon concluded that it would be highly profitable for The Bank of California to open an agency there. He presented his views and was sent back to open and run that office— a branch of the bank that continued in the Washoe hills for the next 53 years.

Sharon was a small, dark, nervous man of unguessed money-making ability. He wore a dangling mustache and a small lip-beard. He dressed in plain black. His only display was a goldheaded cane. When Sharon first reached Virginia City, the railroad had not yet been built from Reno. Heavy freight was brought into town, and ore hauled from mines to mills, on wagons with trailers drawn by teams of twelve or fourteen horses or mules. Fuel, gathered in the surrounding hills, came on donkey-back.

The Bank of California agency was opened for business on the southwest corner of C Street and Taylor. The office was a long, narrow room with an ornate counter making a right angle around a plastered-over iron vault at the rear. There were gas chandeliers in the ceiling. Across the counter of this banking room, for the next five decades, passed a heavy proportion of the business of the Lode.

An agency was also opened in Gold Hill south over the summit of C Street, in May 1865. William Sharon was manager of both offices.

Sharon went to work with energy. The interest rate among the Lode's bankers was five percent per month, sometimes more. Since a bad loan is bad at any

Freighting to the Comstock in the early 1860's.

rate of interest, Sharon picked up the loans he considered most desirable by setting the monthly interest rate at two percent. With funds sent up from San Francisco, he took over the notes of leading properties from lenders too involved to hold them. He provided capital for settling boundary and title disputes and for purchasing new equipment. He, Ralston and Mills entered into some highly profitable personal ventures. His Midas touch was so compelling that Ralston made a private partnership with him in San Francisco real estate and other activities. Mills was invited into some of these projects. When he hesitated, Ralston in certain cases personally guaranteed him against loss. It was a kind of deal that the conservative Mills—or anyone else—could take pleasure in.

Many mills had sprung up to compete for ores from the chain of mines across Virginia City's Mt. Davidson. Every detail of mining and ore reduction was going through a period of trial and error and was often underfinanced. Sharon's analytical mind grasped the importance of gathering in the better mills. Supported by Mills, Ralston, and some others, he brought about the formation of the Union Mill & Mining Company. Mill sites were acquired on Carson River, where old mills were improved and new ones built. The steam mills of the district were unable to compete with the cheaper water power of the river. Union Mill & Mining Company proved to be one of the "bank crowd's" most profitable enterprises. Others were to come, including the Virginia & Truckee Railroad which would tie the Lode in with the oncoming Central Pacific. That was some years in the future.

Sharon's private lodgings were over the Virginia banking room and his talent there for poker with large sums riding on each card soon made startled conversation in that whoopingest mining camp in America. Tales of it were brought to Ralston in San Francisco. "Does Sharon win or lose?" he asked. Told that his agent generally won, "Then I didn't misjudge him," Ralston is reported to have commented.

The Comstock stampede had sent prospectors scurrying all over Nevada in hopes of further finds. One was turned up eastward across the new state at Treasure Hill—a pocket of rich chloride ores. The White Pine District sprang up and when $3,200,000 was removed from an area 70 feet long by 40 feet wide, at a depth nowhere more than 30 feet beneath the surface of the earth, the towns of Hamilton and Treasure City were suddenly famous. They were 3 miles and 1500 vertical feet apart. Treasure City, the higher, was 9,000 feet above the sea. Lumber cost $700 a thousand board feet up there and water was 10 cents a gallon. At the height of the excitement in 1868-9 the two camps claimed populations of six to twelve thousand, schools and churches were built, and The Bank of California opened its "Hamilton" and "White Pine" agencies. Substantial structures were built to house them. But the glittering wealth petered out. The agencies closed down after lasting about a year and a half.

On the Comstock in 1868, mining had a momentary ebb. The early ore bodies

AGENCY

Bank of California,

VIRGINIA, NEVADA.

A. J. RALSTON,   **J. P. MARTIN,**

Agent.   Cashier.

RECEIVE DEPOSITS OF COIN AND BULLION,

Make Collections, Purchase Bullion at the most favorable rates,

AND DO A

GENERAL BANKING BUSINESS.

EXCHANGE FOR SALE ON

PARIS, LONDON, NEW YORK, BANK OF IRELAND, DUBLIN,
SAN FRANCISCO, SACRAMENTO, PORTLAND, OR.,
AND ALL THE PRINCIPAL CITIES.

AGENCY

BANK OF CALIFORNIA,

GOLD HILL, NEVADA.

A. J. RALSTON, Agent.   W. H. BLAUVELT, Cashier.

Receive Deposits of Coin and Bullion, Make Collections, Purchase Bullion at the Most Favorable Rates, and do a

GENERAL BANKING BUSINESS.

EXCHANGE FOR SALE ON

Paris, London, New York, Bank of Ireland, Dublin, San
Francisco, Sacramento, Portland, Oregon,
And all the Principal Cities.

The Virginia City agency of the Bank advertised in the Virginia & Truckee Railroad Directory, 1873-74. William Sharon's rising fortunes had led him to abdicate as the Bank's agent on the Comstock. Andrew J. Ralston assumed management of the Virginia City and Gold Hill agencies.

in Ophir and other properties had ceased to pay and a great body of black sulphurets in Gould & Curry, which had attracted the attention of the world,
seemed to be exhausted. Yet in the depths was unglimpsed ore of such quantity
and richness that it would come to be known as the "Big Bonanza," and startle
the world.

Sharon and associates, by '68, had acquired control of most of the then well-
regarded mines on the Lode. In 1869, however, at the annual meeting of the
stockholders of the Hale & Norcross mine, James Flood and James G. Fair
made their appearance. They held enough stock and proxies to elect the directors. A new power group was rising on the Comstock—Fair, Flood, practical
miner and mine superintendent John W. Mackay, and Flood's cafe partner
William O'Brien.

But soon after, a sensational find was made two miles southward down the
Lode, touching off a frenzy of speculation. This was the uncovering of a large
ore body in Crown Point and Belcher, two mines controlled by Ralston, Sharon
and various friends of the bank.

With these new fountains of treasure on the other side of the Sierra spurting
both silver and gold, William C. Ralston at San Francisco continued investing
heavily in new industries and enterprises for the City and the Coast.

Virginia City Agency of the Bank was in operation from 1864 to 1917.

Ralston and the West

The West was growing. Small but vigorous communities in the Northwest were grouped around the beautiful, deep valleys of Puget Sound. Seattle, a lumbering center, was largest with two score houses. Tacoma was smaller, but was about to be selected for terminus of the proposed Northern Pacific Railroad. In Oregon, farms and towns were spreading in the fertile Willamette Valley. Hundreds of thousands of acres had been broken by the plow.

The bank helped to put many western enterprises on their feet. It gave support to the development of trans-Pacific commerce, and helped lay the basis for the great Oriental trade of the Coast. Ralston was a director of the Contract & Finance Company, builders of the Central Pacific and Southern Pacific railroads. When Leland Stanford was badly in need of $100,000 on his own note for furtherance of the Central Pacific, which was steadily laying rails up and over the Sierra, he had applied to the Pacific Insurance Company for the loan. As one of the insurance company directors, Ralston stood alone in urging that the sum be granted, pledging that The Bank of California would stand behind Stanford's note.

San Francisco in 1864. Drawn and lithographed by C. B. Gifford.

The University of California's first voucher. Drawn on its account at The Bank of California, 1868, by W. C. Ralston, who was both treasurer of the young university and the cashier of the bank.

In 1866 Ralston threw his support behind Adolf Sutro and the proposed Sutro tunnel which would drain and give access at depth to the Comstock mines. When it was realized that control of the tunnel would give control of the Lode, the bank's support was withdrawn. Thereafter Ralston, Sharon, Mills and the Union Mill & Mining Company fought the promoter tooth and nail.

In California, the wheat trade was booming. Western wheat excelled in strength, dryness, whiteness, plumpness and weight. This wheat from the interior valley was an export crop from 1865 onward but required large sums for moving from field to ship. The bank provided it in important amounts. Grain speculation began rivaling the popular interest in mines. Ralston backed an extensive irrigation project for wheat lands. The plan contemplated 900 miles of trunk canals. At Sherman Island where inland rivers met the bay, the immensely valuable peat soil was drained and reclaimed.

The discovery that wheat grew luxuriantly in California was followed by elaborate experiments with other crops. The state realized that it could feed itself and have a margin over. In Sonoma County the Buena Vista Viticultural Society had 6,000 acres planted to wine grapes. Ralston lent a hand to this promising industry.

Experiments were being made in a variety of manufactures. Ralston was interested in a surprising number of them. The big combined Pacific & Mission Woolen mills, 793 feet long, employed 500 people at making blankets, robes, hosiery and clothing material. There were also a Ralston-backed silk factory, a watch factory, a plant that made handsome carriages and railway cars, a furniture factory, a tobacco enterprise at Gilroy employing several thousand Chinese growers and 700 white cigar makers. Recalled Major Charles Lee Tilden, a distinguished pioneer, in a talk on "William C. Ralston and His Times" before the California Historical Society in 1938, "I was secretary of a mining company [in 1875] so they sent me down to The Bank of California. I spent a lot of time going over the books of Mr. Ralston. Those books displayed the most remarkable development of things in the State of California. It is almost impossible to conceive of all those different things he took hold of. In these various things he employed thousands and thousands of men. He was a producer, not a mere money maker."

Ralston and the bank strengthened the California Steam Navigation Company on the inland waterways. Ralston also headed a dry dock company that carved at Hunters Point a basin 421 feet long and 60 feet wide at its bottom, 120 feet at its top, out of solid rock. Twenty-two feet of water lay over its sill at mean tide. It could handle practically any vessel on the Pacific. A floating dry dock, 210 by 82, went in alongside.

Seal fisheries off the Alaskan coast had the benefit of the bank's helping hand. Sealing and fisheries in northern waters led to further reconnaissance that played a role in the State Department's decision to purchase all Alaska from the Russian government. The deal, for $7,200,000, brought to the United States what would become, in time, its forty-ninth state.

Hunters Point Dry Dock with sidewheel steamship *Montana*, in 1869. One of the great dry docks of the country, it played a big role in maritime and naval maintenance in the two world wars of the present century.

The California Theatre. On the Bush Street site now occupied by the Pacific Telephone and Telegraph Company. Bret Harte wrote a poem celebrating its gala opening January 18, 1869, to a crush of 2,479 people. Lawrence Barrett and John McCullough, its managers, provided a stock company of brilliant names. For some years it was San Francisco's largest theatre.

The banker joined in '68 with Asbury Harpending, an operator of soaring imagination himself, in an enterprise known as the Montgomery Street Real Estate Company. Its prime purpose was to open that thoroughfare south of Market Street, This became New Montgomery. The original plan called for driving New Montgomery straight through to Rincon Hill, the center of early social life. That plan was blocked by other landowners. But the company did put up many buildings including, in 1870, the $400,000 Grand Hotel, three quarters Harpending's and one quarter Ralston's. Other plunges, less happy in outcome, were a silver mine called the Emma in Utah, a promotion which victimized many including Ralston; and the immortal Diamond Hoax, perpetrated upon Ralston and others, which resulted in unloading some salted acres in the vicinity of Vermillion Creek in Colorado, on 25 prominent investors of Europe and California. Ralston personally reimbursed those whom he had induced to come in.

It was customary and legal in that day for officers to borrow from their own banks upon good security. The directors knew Ralston was a man of unusual ability and they did not worry. Ralston took a hand in the San Francisco, Oakland & Alameda Railroad Company, combining three small lines of the East Bay. He helped launch the Oakland Water Company. He became treasurer of a more ambitious railroad, the San Francisco & Colorado River, which hoped to extend to Arizona and eastward.

He built, for $225,000, the California Theatre. For some years it was the largest in town, with brilliant names on its stock company roll. Its managers were Lawrence Barrett and John McCullough, famous actors of the time. It opened on January 18, 1869, to a crush of 2,479 people. Bret Harte wrote a poem for the occasion.

Ralston's overflowing energy also found personal expression. He had a home in San Francisco and, 25 miles south at Belmont, a baronial estate. Almost daily, if he didn't go swimming off Hyde Street at the close of banking hours, he mounted the box of a brightly painted tally-ho, gathered the reins of a four-horse team in one hand, cocked a whip in the other, and was off with distinguished guests or a company of friends for his home down the Peninsula, racing any train that challenged. Relays of fresh horses awaited with hostlers at the bits, and the engineers of the 30-ton San Francisco & San Jose locomotives ate mouthfuls of carriage dust. The estate at Belmont was a place of rose-lined

The nation had never seen anything like it — the bay-windowed Palace Hotel, almost twice as large as any other in its day; two and a half miles of corridors, a fireplace in every room, carpets by the acre, tubs for 437 bathrooms, 850 guest rooms, 20 miles of gas pipe, 8 miles of steam pipe, a promenade of one-third of a mile on top of the seven stories; a balconied and roofed-over central court into which carriages could drive. The boilers, salvaged after the quake and fire of 1906, today heat nine glassed-in acres of orchids and gardenias near Colma.

walks, long greenhouses, a private gas plant, saddle and carriage horses, and seventeen-course dinners. In the mansion of mirrors and chandeliers, Mrs. Ralston and he gave many balls and dinners. The Ralston home is now the College of Notre Dame, with its high school. He was host to all important California visitors, a one-man chamber of commerce. The tireless man was also a pioneer and dedicated regent of the young University of California. The first voucher it ever issued was drawn upon The Bank of California by Ralston as the university's treasurer.

As a young girl, Gertrude Atherton, the California authoress, knew Ralston. Her grandfather was Secretary Franklin of the bank. Mr. Ralston often came to her home. Her memory in after years was of a thick-set man with a massive face, clean-shaven about the mouth, and not too much beard; with a piercing but kind and often humorous eye, a firm mouth which occasionally relaxed into a spontaneous and charming smile, and a cast-iron repose. She sensed that the granite exterior surrounded a dynamo and in retrospect decided that it encased an often insupportable tension. No other man was so admired and trusted. And, she added, no man ever had a better time. He loved power, work, excitement and variety.

In the opening '70's he decided to lay at the feet of his city his greatest token of devotion: a hotel frankly designed to be the largest in the world. Here should be comfort and grandeur never before known to travelers.

Architects were summoned, plans drawn, ground broken in 1872. The Grand Pacific Hotel in Chicago had 58,000 square feet, the Palmer House 56,000, and one in New York 36,000, but the Palace was to have 96,000 square feet—nearly double the largest in the country. It would occupy a full block on Market Street and would cost, with furnishings, $5 million. Anything it needed would be ordered. If the article wasn't available, a factory would be built to make it.

Sharon, his partner in this and many other personal ventures, was awed by it all. If Ralston wanted a plank, Sharon protested, purchase was made of a whole forest.

But for the city that was Ralston's religion, nothing could be too splendid. And as a businessman, he was certain that his great hotel would pay its way many-fold.

Meanwhile, trade with the Orient must be encouraged; the steamer and windjammer lanes must be kept busy. Commerce was the lifeblood of the Coast and the bank was the heart that pumped the lifeblood. Daily, Ralston saw everyone, hiding any worries that gnawed him. His energy, the sweep of his plans fascinated his associates and fellow townsmen. Sharon later observed: "If he got into anything there was no end to it. He never beat a retreat until he struck the ocean."

Regularly, for a restorative dip in the waves, Ralston continued to turn to that ocean. He did this at the end of many a busy day.

Era of Dizzy Speculation

As the 1870's dawned, all citizens of both Nevada and California, it seemed, were trying to make money in the stock market. "Some," said a broker of the time, "were content with a reasonable profit, say a hundred per cent in a few days or a few weeks."

The San Francisco Stock and Exchange Board was the *Big Board* among three exchanges and a seat came to be worth $30,000. Crowds outside were sometimes so dense that teams couldn't pass. Almost everyone was in the "market"—lawyers, doctors, merchants, clerks, hod carriers. Women joined the mania. Some visited their brokers by private entrances. Others surged in the streets, or jammed the visitors' gallery at the *Big Board*. An unchivalrous name —"mudhens"—was coined for them. Leidesdorff Street between California and Pine was dubbed "Pauper Alley" in behalf of those whom Lady Luck eluded. Though many decades have passed and many bricks fallen, "Pauper Alley" it still is to those who cherish tradition.

Behind the fire apparatus, the huge U. S. Mint that turned out hundreds of millions in gold coin, saved the banks of San Francisco from delay in resuming business after the 1906 quake and fire, and in later years made copper pennies.

Panorama of Virginia City showing extensive mining operations

With his intimate knowledge of the Comstock's seesawing fortunes, William Sharon followed matters closely. When ore of great promise had been found in Crown Point, he had made up his mind that the mine adjoining it on the south would have its share. He had bought Best & Belcher on behalf of himself and associates and it went from $100 a share to $2,000. He was able to tell his broker that he was the second richest man in Nevada or California, just behind D. O. Mills.

The experienced eyes of James G. Fair and John W. Mackay led that pair to conclude that great finds also lay well to the north of Belcher and Crown Point. They convinced their San Francisco partners, Flood and O'Brien, and took over neglected claims between the latest bonanza and Ophir, the Comstock's discovery mine. The world-famous Consolidated Virginia Mining Company was incorporated to hold and develop these gathered-up claims. From part of its ground was organized the equally famous California Mining Company.

During these years the active management of the bank had remained in the hands of William C. Ralston. Mr. Mills was often absent, arranging connections and correspondents for the bank abroad.

A wave of failures and bank runs brought on an almost complete stoppage of business east of the Rocky Mountains, and the virtual paralysis of money markets on that side of the divide. The catastrophe was slow making itself felt in the Far West. The rise of agriculture, notably the great gains in wheat production; the booming overseas commerce; and the fact that here gold and silver were the media of exchange, all served to postpone the day of reckoning. Railroads continued to be financed and built. New steamship lines were put into operation. At San Francisco, impressive buildings went up on the downtown streets, more factories rose, and Nob Hill began to be crowned with mansions. But the titanic operations of the Nevada mines dominated business life. As money lenders, the commercial banks were considerably involved with the speculative trend. They accepted the stocks as collateral under an agreement permitting sale without notice so as to protect themselves against serious declines.

To again quote Major Charles L. Tilden's vivid reminiscences* years afterward:

It was a gambling age—it was an age of speculation. How can I say it to you? You folks think you know something about speculation and gambling. You know what happened in 1929 and 1930. Everybody was gambling but not like it was in the early days in San Francisco in the late sixties and early seventies. Why, I let a man have $200 because he had to pay an assessment on some mining stock. He couldn't pay his assessments. There were many of them. So I let him have $200 for 1,000 shares. Within sixty days I sold it for over $5,000. I wanted to know how long that sort of thing had been going on. Everybody in San Francisco was doing the same thing. It was contagious. Lots were being purchased, lots were being given away for, say, five dollars, and then sold again for, say, fifty dollars, and after a while the same lot would sell for a hundred, and then five hundred, and then a thousand. Not that they were worth anything, but a fellow paid $500 because he thought he could sell for a thousand. The same thing, too, with mining stock. I think Crown Point was selling at some time as low as ten cents, or so, a share, and it went up to a tremendous advance of two dollars a share. What percentage of profit was that? . . .

In the old days banks were not conducted as at the present time when anybody borrowing, has to file a statement in detail, and tell everything he owns in the world, even tell all about his wife and whether she has anything, what he is going to do with the money and this, and that and the other thing. In the old days they did not do business like that. Men would walk into the bank, it didn't make much difference what bank, and would say, "Hello, Bill, I want to have some money." "How much money do you want?" "I want a credit of $50,000. I guess that will carry me for a while." "All right, Jim, just draw your checks." Didn't sign any note or any statement, just had overdrafts. That was just a matter of course, a matter of honor and standing. . . .

On January 15, 1873, D. O. Mills, feeling pressure of other affairs, resigned

---

*Talk delivered by Major Tilden at a luncheon in Hotel Sir Francis Drake, San Francisco, April 12, 1938, on the subject "William C. Ralston and His Times."

from the bank's presidency and also from the board of directors. Ralston succeeded to the presidency, his place as cashier being filled by the promotion of Thomas Brown.

In the summer of 1874, The Bank of California could look back on ten years of existence. Its stock had long sold for $150 above par; dividends of one percent had been paid regularly on the 15th of each month. A contemporary financial writer observed: "Starting under the favorable auspices of a strong organization, and with a capital so large for that period, the bank's career during the following decade more than fulfilled the brightest hopes of its founders."

In the opening weeks of '74, rumors relating to Con Virginia and its neighbors had been followed by wide fluctuations on the stock market. By midspring it was definitely known that an important discovery had been made. How great this "big bonanza" was to prove—and it proved staggering—was anybody's guess. Philip Deidesheimer, an accepted expert, went down into Consolidated Virginia and came up blinking. He pronounced that the metal in sight was worth at least a billion and a half. He was supported in this opinion by a Director of the Mint. The lump extended from Con Virginia into California and perhaps, at greater depth, into Ophir. The battle for control was on. "Bank crowd" and "bonanza kings" were locked in combat. The public was swept in with them.

As 1874 ended, shrewd observers began to fear that the hard times being felt in the East were bound to reach the Coast. There had been a sharp decline in the price of silver, which Congress had demonitized. Realization was growing that Comstock shares had been bid up far beyond possible worth. But for most of the public, the giddy pace could never end. Millionaires and sand-shovelers, businessmen and gamblers, waiters, bankers, Chinese laundrymen, butcher boys, cab-drivers, all were caught in the speculative whirl that, by this time, was as characteristic of the town as the sea fogs blowing in through its harbor gate.

"The people are crazy," reported a San Francisco eye-witness to the *Union* at Sacramento. "Yesterday and today, when California was jumping at $10 a bid, the frenzy of the crowd reached its height. The rush to get in was wild, enthusiastic and reckless. Brokers were almost beside themselves, while men and women rushed frantically about, issuing orders and eagerly scanning the lists and straining to catch the bids on the street."

On and up indeed roared Con Virginia, California and Ophir. At the turn of the year the total market price for the three equalled the assessed value of all the real estate in San Francisco, and no top was in sight.

Con Virginia, $160 a share not long before, was $705. California, lately $89, stood at $790. At this price one could put in $60,000 and it bought just ten inches along the Washoe fissure. Every clerk or stevedore who held a knifeblade's thickness of ownership saw himself a new Monte Cristo who shortly

The San Francisco Stock Exchange in Pine Street, nerve center of the speculative mining era, was eagerly watched from all the cities of America and Europe as Crown Point and Yellow Jacket, Con. Virginia and California, Ophir and Savage and Mexican and the other mines of the mighty Comstock made millionaires and paupers.

would sit with Sharon, Ralston, Baldwin, Mills and Hayward, or perhaps on the cloud-wreathed summit with Fair, Mackay, Flood and O'Brien.

In Chicago the *Inter-Ocean* marveled: "No city upon this continent can show more men of solid wealth than San Francisco. Mines of fabulous possibilities pour their dividends. . . . Many of her citizens could sell out at a month's notice for $5,000,000 each. Palaces have risen from silver bricks, and the proudest buildings in the city owe their origin to ores and bullion."

"Worth $5,000,000!" the San Francisco *Chronicle* jeered. "These are only our 'well-to-do' citizens, men of 'comfortable' incomes—our middle class. . . . In a small interior village like Chicago a man worth a million is esteemed wealthy. Not so in the grand commercial emporium of the Pacific. We do not call a person wealthy unless he advances beyond the tens of millions. Next year we will speak of those who possess hundreds of millions."

"Next year"—1875—was just around the corner.

Ophir Hoisting Works, Virginia City

The Doors Close and Reopen

The morning of Thursday, August 26, 1875, was hot and sticky, the kind of day that after 1906 would be called by San Franciscans, "earthquake weather." Readers of the *Alta* noted that in mining stocks "yesterday was the severest day ever experienced in California, and that it will pass into history as the 'Black Wednesday' of San Francisco. . . . This sudden change in the Stock Market would indicate that a great battle is raging among the giants." Ophir in one day declined from $59 to $17, Con Virginia from $62 to $6, and others as savagely.

At The Bank of California, tellers brought their gold from the vault as usual. The coins gave a mellow chink. But Cashier Brown looked at them in foreboding: the supply of coin available in town was dangerously small. Last January 1, there had been $20 million of it in circulation in the city. On August 1, there was only $14,250,000, a drop of nearly one-third. The San Francisco Mint was

California Street looked like this in 1878. The Bank of California at right center.

currently not coining any gold or silver and the unusually large wheat crop of the interior was being harvested and moved, draining off $4 million more. With nerves jumpy over the stock market and a falling price of silver, and the lash of the East's panic of '73 at last being felt on the Coast, withdrawals of cash had been heavy all week. Its possessors were hoarding. Brokers were locking up funds in their office safes. All banking houses reported extreme difficulty in collecting loans.

But the sight of President Ralston in his office through his open door was reassuring. Mr. Ralston was always the picture of optimism. Difficulties did not daunt him. Mr. Sharon and Mr. Mills were also at personal desks in the building; Mr. Mills had recently returned to the city.

In the first hour or two, the paying tellers were busy but not acutely so. Then, toward noon, ominous word spread through the financial district. A broker who regularly represented Mr. Sharon had gone on the floor of the Stock & Exchange Board and was executing apparently unlimited selling orders on Comstock shares. Was this in order to raise urgently needed cash for The Bank of California? Rumor swelled. By ones and twos, the bank's customers pressed in. At two o'clock the lines extended from counter to doors. More trays of gold coin were brought from the vault, and more. Withdrawals were met as rapidly as possible. "Lucky" Baldwin, who was building a rival hotel to Ralston's Palace and who had $750,000 on deposit, gallantly refused to take out a penny. But some of the withdrawals were very large. All the conditions that can cause a major run were rushing toward a common point like the whirling winds of a typhoon. The rivalries of the Comstock; the jealousies of moneyed titans in battle for power; recent assaults by a part of the daily press and a dozen other unrelated but adverse circumstances were concentrating upon Ralston and his extended position. Ralston's last-ditch sources failed him. Twenty minutes before the 3 o'clock closing hour, he was forced to give the signal. Payments were suspended. Later that day Secretary Franklin, with a shaky hand for the first time in his career, penned in the Minutes of the Board, "4 P.M. Mr. Ralston in the chair stated to the Board that after the most strenuous efforts to obtain coin to carry on the business of the Bank, it had been compelled to close its doors."

The next day, after a hectic twenty-four hours that had ended in his resignation being demanded and accepted, William C. Ralston walked out of the bank. He took the horse-cars to the water's edge in the vicinity of Hyde Street, where there was a public bath house he frequently patronized. He chatted briefly with the proprietor, and went for his usual swim. He was seen to be in physical difficulty. A youth in a boat went to his rescue. Resuscitation efforts on the beach were well-meant but clumsy, ending in tragic failure.

Heart failure, or suicide? A coroner's autopsy did not specify. It found in the lungs "No water in quantity sufficient to be recognized," which many persons accepted to mean that the sudden plunge into chilly sea water, in that hour of intense strain, had been fatal to the powerful heart and constitution. "Mr. Ralston went down like a giant Sequoia," remembered Major Tilden in his address previously quoted.

Ralston died at 49 years of age. An estimated 50,000 people watched the funeral and many followed it through the streets. It was a remarkable testimonial of affection for the man whose warmth and whose plans for his city and the West had been so extensive.

Five days after the closing, a committee headed by William Sharon set about raising subscriptions from stockholders "with the sole object of supplying a fund for the relief of the bank when needed." Mills and Sharon led off with pledges of $1 million each. E. J. "Lucky" Baldwin pledged the same amount. The San Francisco Stock and Exchange Board subscribed $250,000. Opposite the names of dozens, from $10,000 to $150,000 was set down. The total amount pledged was $7,895,000, a sum twice what was ultimately called in. Earnest

One of the most popular financiers in the development of the early West, William C. Ralston was memorialized in this manner by the *News Letter*, a San Francisco weekly.

pressure was put upon D. O. Mills to head the bank again, until it got well under way. His reputation for being a cool-headed, unemotional, conservative banker in whom the public had implicit confidence made him the man for the task, and he accepted it. Thomas Brown continued as cashier.

By the end of September, to the enormous relief of San Francisco and the financial world, the date for resuming business was announced. Once again Secretary Franklin took his pen in hand and wrote in round script, "Sept. 30, 1875. On motion of Mr. Sharon it was Resolved, that the President be and he is hereby authorized to open the Bank for business Saturday next the 2nd day of October at the usual hour, and that the agencies in Virginia City, Gold Hill and New York be instructed to open at the same hour."

October 2, 1875, was a memorable day. The opening of the Coast's leading bank, on a firmer basis than before and with public confidence stronger than ever, took on the aspect of a city-wide holiday. Plans were made to serenade the bank's officers at the hour of the opening, but these were abandoned at the latters' request. At an early hour crowds assembled on California Street until traffic was all but suspended. Previous to the opening, men carrying bags of coin were admitted through a wicket door. Within, every officer and attache was at his post. A half million dollar solid pile of twenty-dollar gold pieces was on the counter, the advance guard of two millions more lying in the vaults. As the clock in the nearby Merchants Exchange tower struck ten, flags were run up above buildings along the financial streets and in all parts of the city. An artillery salute was fired from Telegraph Hill. The doors swung open; customers filed in. Several claimed the honor of making the first deposit and wrote heated letters about it afterward to the newspapers. The results of the first day's business was: deposits, $1,020,000; withdrawals, $254,000.

Zoeth T. Eldredge, the historian who was there, wrote of the bank in after decades:

The prestige of its name, the romance of its history and the hold it had on the imagination of the people, the character of the men in control, the large amount of its syndicate guaranty as well as the strength and standing of its guarantors, all told in its favor, and proved the perfect success of the rehabilitation—a success more wonderful than was dreamed of by the managers—for, from being the great bank of the state, The Bank of California had become one of the great banks of the nation.

On the day the bank reopened, the city also celebrated another event: the opening of the newly completed Palace Hotel. William Sharon, speaking to the throng from a balcony of the Grand Court, called the day the beginning of a new era in San Francisco's history.

With The Bank of California soundly rehabilitated by its stockholders and other well-wishers, the stock exchanges also reopened. But the feverish speculation that had marked the board's activities over the Big Bonanza was slowed down. Suddenly Virginia City was completely devastated by fire. The town immediately rebuilt but its "wild and woolly" era was over, and Comstock mines which had been valued on the market at $300 million in January, '75, were down to $7 million in 1881.

The worldwide commerce in and out of San Francisco continued to be served well by the bank. Its financial backing and instruments of exchange helped to dispatch the grain, the canned foods, the timber and mineral products of the West, and to land cargoes from China, India, the South Seas, the Americas and Europe.

In 1876, a new wonder-working invention, the telephone, was announced and demonstrated. San Francisco had its first telephone exchange in 1878, that of the Gold & Stock Telegraph Co., at 222 Sansome Street not far from the bank. By 1906 the Pacific Telephone and Telegraph Company had been formed out of predecessor companies. From early times, The Bank of California has been closely associated with Coast telephone development.

D. O. Mills held the presidency of the bank until May, 1878, when he felt justified in relinquishing it. He transferred his personal activities to New York, where he conducted large interests and philanthropies. He retained one of his homes at Millbrae, a dozen miles south of San Francisco. He died there in 1910 at the age of 84.

Upon D. O. Mills' retirement from his second presidency of the bank, William Alvord succeeded him. Alvord arrived in California from New York in 1853, while in his early twenties. He had established in San Francisco a leading importing and wholesale firm, had helped organize the Risdon Iron Works among many other activities, and had served as the city's mayor.

In 1876 San Francisco's first clearing house was organized. It was a major step toward cooperation among the banks of the state. At this time, banks still could be established with as little as ten percent of the capital paid in. Promissory notes without security often made up the rest. There was no state inspection of banks. Reserves, capitalization and banking practices were still without fixed standards. Anyone still could set up as a private banker. But popular demand forced adoption of a new state constitution. A three-man commission was set up to examine and supervise the state banks. It was a sign that the West was outgrowing its carefree ways.

The 1880's in California provided less drama, but solid growth. The Central Pacific and its connection, the Union Pacific, had wrought great changes. A second line east, the Southern Pacific, was completed from San Francisco to New Orleans and a third, the Santa Fe, was constructed. The southern part of California experienced a railroad rate war during which, on one hectic day, transportation of colonists from Kansas City to Los Angeles was sold for a dollar a head.

Historic Colgate Powerhouse on the North Fork of the Yuba River east of Marysville. Built in 1899, this plant was the first Sierra hydroelectric powerhouse to transmit electricity to the San Francisco Bay Area in 1901, when a 142-mile line was built to Oakland in a remarkable feat of engineering for that time.

The emphasis was turning from gold and silver mining to agriculture and industry in ever greater degree. Barley, grapes and citrus fruits were expanding their acreage. Miscellaneous mining was on the rise, including borax, copper, cement. Petroleum had been noticed in pioneer days in Southern California. During the 1880's, 3 million barrels were produced. During the '90's, production rose to 11 million barrels and the state was on its way to becoming an important producer of "black gold." By 1906, California's oil production would surpass that of metallic gold in value.

Hydroelectric power had its state beginnings at Pomona with a 13-mile transmission line of 5,000 voltage. In 1894, predecessors of Pacific Gas & Electric Co. began hydroelectric transmission in Northern California. The 1900 Census was able to declare, "Electric current is transmitted from the Sierras in Eastern California as far as San Francisco and other cities adjacent to the Pacific seacoast," and bracket the development with that of Niagara Falls. "White gold" —hydroelectric power—had arrived on the Coast.

Petroleum and electric power were to play a huge part in offsetting the West's manufacturing disadvantages of high costs for labor and material.

Fiscal affairs in San Francisco still were settled twice a month on "Steamer Day." The name was rooted in the traditions of '49 and the '50's, when steamships had left regularly twice a month with gold dust and instruments of exchange, and all accounts in the seaport city were supposed to be settled and clean slates started on each 13th and 28th day. In earlier times it had been the custom for banks to keep open until 10 P.M. on these collection dates, in order to accommodate buyers of exchange on New York; and sometimes it was 2 A.M. before the weary clerks and tellers left for home. Until the 1900's, "Steamer Day" saw collectors going about gathering coin in bags until their shoulders sagged. Personal checking accounts still were rare in the '80's and "banking by mail" was as unthought-of as space ships.

At The Bank of California, where in 1879 deposits had been $6 million and resources $11,280,000, the increase in deposits during the '80's was almost 50 percent.

There were few inventions as yet to lighten labor and shorten hours in the business world. There were no adding machines—clearings, receiving tellers' deposits and all the rest—were added by hand. The Bank of California's first telephone went into the office of the bank's land agent. Then came a booth phone at the back of the bank. Cashier Brown abhorred using it and delegated message-taking to his assistant. When the bank acquired its first woman employee, around 1890, she came in as a telephone operator. Later she became the bank's first stenographer. Her name is apparently lost to the record. What a future array she spearheaded!

By the mid-nineties, there were 4 million bicycles on the roads of America, and a handful of motor cars. Congress had been inspired to vote $10,000 to the Secretary of Agriculture to look into the subject of better roads. The $50 billion network of new highways currently repaving America is a descendant of that initial $10,000. But the first credit for it goes to the bike. The *Literary Digest* was still assuring its readers, in 1899, "The ordinary 'horse-less carriage' is at present a luxury for the wealthy; and although its price will probably fall in the future, it will never, of course, come into as common use as the bicycle."

In San Francisco, the click of car-cables, the cheerful clang of gong, the conductor's "Koutferthecurve" had become the voice of the city. The softly slapping cables ran up and down most of the hills and in the level streets too. The gripmen were athletic fellows greatly admired by small boys.

The nineteenth century ended, and The Bank of California decided to expand. Its attention turned to the Pacific Northwest.

Broadway Wharf, 1890, received merchandise from all over the world, that supplied San Francisco's growing population

The Bank Pushes Northward

The first important American migration to the Coast was not that of the gold rush to California, but was the steady westward flow of wagons and settlers by the Oregon Trail to homestakes along and south of the Columbia River. Astoria, the first permanent American foothold in the Pacific Northwest, had been founded as a trading post for John Jacob Astor's Pacific Fur Company in 1811.

In '43 a considerable wagon train rolled in and a provisional government was set up in the Willamette Valley. The British-American boundary was established at the 49th parallel after hot dispute; the village of Portland acquired its first school; and by 1848 Oregon Territory had been established by Congress. The more than 300,000 square miles were later carved up into the states of Oregon, Washington, Idaho, and parts of Montana and Wyoming.

Homeseekers who came by the Oregon Trail found the Willamette Valley fertile and inviting. With rifles handy and eyes peeled for Indians, they started rolling back the forests and breaking the soil to the plow. By 1850 the Territory claimed 13,294 white population. Nine years later, word reached Portland that the Oregon of present-day boundaries had been admitted to the Union as a State.

Night view showing Tacoma's newest landmark, the dominating The Bank of California neon sign.

Immigration also had reached the southern end of Puget Sound. There were settlements on Elliott Bay and at the tip of Olympic Peninsula. Washington became a Territory of that name in 1853, while still including the present northern Idaho and western Montana. Its white population was 3,965.

In 1851, some wagon-train pioneers from Illinois, by way of Portland, had reached Olympia and from there sailed northward down the Sound. From Alki Point, now within Seattle's boundaries, David Denny sent word to his brother at Portland, "Come as soon as you can. We have found a valley that will support a thousand families." By '54 the town had 8 houses, a church, and a school. Catherine E. Blaine, the minister's wife, conducted the school. Its site today, at First Avenue and Columbia, is occupied by the three-story garage and customers' parking facility of The Bank of California, whose office is at 815 Second Avenue.

Tacoma, on Commencement Bay halfway between Olympia and Seattle, also had its beginnings in the early 1850's. Nicholas De Lin cleared land and set up a water-driven sawmill. He shipped 550,000 board feet of lumber to San Francisco on the brig *George Emory*, and the little hamlet close under Mount Rainier was started to becoming the woodworking capital of the world.

Throughout the 1870's and early 1880's a remarkable development took place

The City of Portland as it appeared about 1880.

in the Pacific Northwest. The products of its lumber mills, fisheries, and, in particular, its great wheat ranches, became important factors in the world's markets. It was largely to finance the movement of wheat from the Columbia Basin to Europe that the London & San Francisco Bank, on February 1, 1882, established a branch at Portland. This was followed by branches at Tacoma and Seattle. As the business of the head office and all three branches of the London & San Francisco Bank was taken over by The Bank of California in 1905, the antecedents of that bank and the early careers of its three northwest branches will be described.

In 1865, eight months after The Bank of California began business, the English banking house known as the London & San Francisco Bank, Ltd., entered the West Coast field. Its two American agencies were in New York and San Francisco, the latter under the management of Milton S. Latham, at 412 Montgomery Street. Latham was a notable social and political figure, for many years prominent in San Francisco financial circles. He had been a Congressman, governor of California, and a U. S. Senator.

At the outset, London & San Francisco Bank was interested chiefly in the

Interior of The Bank of California in the Chamber of Commerce Building, 3rd and Stark Streets, Portland, until removal to SW 6th and Stark in 1925.

purchase and shipment of bullion, and making loans on securities, merchandise, and precious metals, and issuing letters of credit. Six years after its founding, it absorbed the banking business of Parrott and Company. This private bank had been founded by John Parrott in 1855. Mr. Parrott, one of the strong financial figures of pioneer times, had erected substantial masonry buildings, carried his bank through panics, and served his city well.

The first Portland office of London & San Francisco Bank was in the Ainsworth Building on S. W. Third Avenue and Oak Street. It was opened under the management of William Mackintosh, a durable financial figure esteemed throughout the Northwest. Portland's population was then about 17,500; with its suburbs, perhaps 30,000. As with other banks in Portland in the eighties and nineties, the staff was tiny and its banking methods simple. It was the era of the huge ledger, stand-up desk, and high stool; of swinging coattails, tall hats, wood stove and kerosene lamp. Specimen signatures of customers were kept in a big leather-backed book which still exists. The names in it are those closely identified with Portland's and Oregon's history.

In 1884 the London & San Francisco Bank moved to its own building at 48 First Avenue. There it remained until during the high water of June, 1894. At this time the bank was moved to dry quarters in the Chamber of Commerce Building, which had entrances on 3rd, 4th and Stark streets.

In the panic year 1893, runs closed eight Portland banks. Three that weathered the storm — banks ample in resources but short of cash — obtained $500,000 in gold by special train from San Francisco, and it came from The Bank of California. The London & San Francisco Bank, Ltd., was one of the three survivors of this disastrous period.

In Portland and throughout the Northwest Mr. Mackintosh had become recognized as the dean of bankers, his sturdy character and full beard making him a notable personality. In 1905, when The Bank of California acquired the business of the London & San Francisco, Mr. Mackintosh was put in general supervision of the branches at Portland, Tacoma and Seattle.

Tacoma's importance had greatly increased when reconnaissance started for the Northern Pacific Railroad. In 1872 a committee from that corporation cruised the Puget Sound area in search of a tidewater terminal site for the proposed 2,000-mile line from Minnesota. Tacoma had only a sawmill and a few houses, backed by a forest wilderness, but level land was ample and the shores fronted deep water of endless extent. A magnificent mountain looked down. The site was selected and a company was formed to lay out a city and sell its lots and wharf privileges.

The railroad started building at both ends, western construction beginning at Kalama on the Columbia and reaching Tacoma in '73. The Northern Pacific

The City of Seattle in 1873

soon ran trains through from Puget Sound to Kalama and thence up the Columbia gorge and eastward. It was the nation's second "transcontinental." In '87,
by means of switchbacks up and over the Cascades, it put Tacoma on a more
direct route. But Henry Villard, who had captured control of Northern Pacific
in the early '80's and completed it, had put its main freight terminal at Seattle.
When James J. Hill drove his Great Northern through, he too terminated it at
Seattle.

These events and the general hard times of the 1890's should have flattened
the city on Commencement Bay, but they didn't. With the rich produce of
Puyallup Valley, the incredible forests, all that level land at the head of deep-
draft navigation, and 33 miles of waterfront, Tacoma grew.

Into this city in 1899, when it had 21 banks for a population of 36,000, came
a branch of the London and San Francisco Bank, Ltd. The bank opened with
three employees. Premises were a storeroom in the Mason Block, also known
as the Ferry Building, 1009 A Street. Two years later the Bank moved to the
French Building at Pacific Avenue and 13th Street; still later to the Luzon
Building across Pacific. Two more moves were to come: to the Fidelity Building at Broadway and 11th in 1919, and to the present location on Pacific a
few years later.

When the business of London & San Francisco Bank was acquired by The
Bank of California, the city had bank clearings of $165 million a year, and an

ocean commerce of $40 million. It was approaching 100,000 in population. The Tacoma staff and office passed to the new banner but remained exactly what they had been: long-time or native Tacomans, operating a bank in the way Tacomans were used to. The only noticeable change was the greatly increased lending capacity. This became an important factor in developing Tacoma industry and business.

A momentous day for Seattle was July 17, 1897, when the "gold ship"

The Bank's Tacoma (Washington) Office.
A $750,000 expansion and remodeling project was begun in June, 1964.

Present Portland, Oregon Office. A full city block has been acquired near our present location with construction of a new building slated to begin in 1965.

Portland of the Pacific Steam Whaling Company arrived in Elliott Bay with $384,000 in newly-discovered treasure from Alaska. Newspaper reports spread east that a "ton of gold" had arrived. The U.S. was recovering from the depression of the nineties and gold fever swept men's minds. Thousands of adventurers rushed to Seattle. "Klondike" and "Nome" became magic words. Gold receipts at Seattle reached a peak in 1901. By that time, trade with Alaska and the Canadian Yukon was firmly a part of Seattle's economy. The last year of the old century found the city with 80,000 people. A dozen banks were in operation. From 1898 until 1914, $227,500,000 in gold was received at the U.S. assay office in Seattle. Alaskan fisheries and furs were also creating new wealth, much of which passed through Seattle or stayed there. Between 1890 and 1900, the total deposits in the city's banks jumped from $1,800,000 to $12,350,000.

This was the city in which London and San Francisco Bank, Ltd., in 1901 opened its fourth Coast office. The spirit of Seattle, raw and vigorous and stimulating, strongly suggested that of San Francisco of fifty years before.

The office of this early-day Seattle bank was at First Avenue and Cherry, a block from Yesler Way, which was originally a logging road. Later it moved to Second and Cherry. This was the location when The Bank of California absorbed the office in 1905.

Since that date more than a half century ago, the three Northwest branches have not only grown with Oregon and Washington, but have greatly assisted the economy supporting that growth. There have been times when the loans of one or another of the branches have exceeded deposits. The strength of the head office has always been back of the Northwest offices, which in turn have frequently furnished top executives to the bank as a whole. The three Northwest offices each are major banks in their own right. Some 30 percent of the entire Bank of California's total deposits are today held by them. Despite the fact that these Washington and Oregon branches are "one-office" operations, not assisted by branches within their respective states, their deposit growth in the last ten years has kept pace with the expansion of total deposits in all banks in those states.

WILLIAM ALVORD
3rd President, The Bank of California,
1878-1905.

HOMER S. KING
4th President, The Bank of California,
1905-1909.

Quake, Fire and Steady Growth

At San Francisco, the bank had outgrown the bluestone seams which had been stitched around it nearly four decades before. In 1905, additional land was purchased on both sides of the familiar California-Sansome corner and Bliss & Faville, prominent architects, were commissioned to plan an adequate and suitable new structure. The program called for demolishing the old building completely. Arrangements were made for interim occupancy of the California-Leidesdorff corner, the building formerly used by the London & San Francisco Bank.

In January, 1906, the bank moved its books and business the short block west to Leidesdorff. Wreckers went to work on the building that had been a landmark for two generations. The site was cleared, the granite quarried and cut.

Left of fire engine, the site vacated by The Bank of California building of 1867 in order to make room for the structure opened in 1908. The black smoke of the great city-wide fire billows over lower California Street and the Embarcadero.

Looking up California Street from a walltop above Sansome Street
St. Francis Hotel on the far left, Fairmont Hotel high on right.

The night of April 17 was warm and fine. "The gayest, lightest-hearted, most pleasure-loving city on the western continent, and in many ways the most interesting and romantic," as Will Irwin soon would write for the New York *Sun*, enjoyed as usual its promenade of the "cocktail route" down Market and Kearny, up Sutter and down Powell. At the Grand Opera House, Caruso and other international stars performed, and at the Mechanics Pavilion—soon to be an emergency morgue—a masked carnival was held on roller skates. The staffs of the three morning papers went home after midnight, their day's work done. At around 2:00 A.M., April 18, 1906, the presses started running. The editions streamed off, crisp and folded, in time for San Francisco breakfast tables. They weren't delivered. Instead, the presses of the Oakland *Tribune* issued a combined Call-Chronicle-Examiner with a headline screaming what hundreds of thousands already knew—EARTHQUAKE AND FIRE: SAN FRANCISCO IN RUINS.

The quake was hundreds of square miles in extent, tumbling chimneys and buildings in town after town, but fire came to San Francisco with the breaking of the distributing mains leading from the city's water supply. Immediately after the first shock at 5:13 A.M., the fires started in uncounted places. In those first hours, three Bank of California employees, Wally Beanston of the foreign department and Marshall Baldwin and Billy Connor, bookkeepers, made their way down town over fallen bricks to the bank's temporary home. They gathered up everything that seemed valuable, including the signature book and other documents, and crowded them between the outer and inner doors of the vault.

Fire destroyed 490 blocks of built-up property, including the financial, wholesale and retail sections. Some 250,000 people were made homeless. Many lives were lost. Food was rushed from nearby cities. The railroads carried thousands away while 100,000 camped in the parks and vacant lots.

The banks, commercial and savings, held $439,000,000 of the people's money. The fire had sealed every bank vault. It would be unsafe to open them for at least three weeks. To let oxygen in sooner would cause combustible contents to leap into flame. A meeting of the San Francisco Clearing House Association was called by President Homer S. King, who was also then president of The Bank of California, to devise ways and means to relieve the people during the acute shortage of money. He was notably assisted by Frank A. Leach, superintendent of the San Francisco Mint. The U.S. Mint building at Fifth and Mission streets had not been destroyed internally. An artesian water supply of its own, and heroic work by employees, had saved the structure, which contained some $300 million in gold. In no other building on the Coast and perhaps in the entire country was so much real money in storage. Leach wired to the Secretary of the Treasury, "Every bank in San Francisco buried in ruins. All banks in Oakland, Berkeley and Alameda able to resume business. To meet the conditions, the suburban banks ought to have free and prompt telegraphic transfer of funds. In view of the ruined condition of the sub-treasury, I advise making the transfer direct through the mint." The suggestion was adopted.

For a half year after the fire The Bank of California's office was in the Loughborough Mansion, Franklin and O'Farrell. A life insurance company, a dentist and several lawyers shared the edifice.

Fire gutted temporary quarters of the Bank, first occupied January 1906 while permanent site was being cleared for construction of present Head Office.

Thousands of people were benefitted. A person or firm in the East desiring to have a sum of money delivered to a person, firm or corporation in San Francisco, or any part of the state would deposit the amount at any of the sub-treasuries in the United States, giving the name and address of the person to whom it was to be delivered. These particulars would be telegraphed to the mint superintendent, and he would notify the beneficiaries to come and get the money.

At Superintendent Leach's invitation, the leading banks set up a central bank within the Mint. For many days, through this temporary combining of forces, the banking business of the city centered in the rugged building. Each bank looked after its own depositors, and was permitted to advance to them such sums as might be necessary.

As soon as the general banking organization at the Mint was a going affair, President King opened a branch of The Bank of California in his own home at 1895 Broadway. At the same time, an improvised downtown structure for the bank was knocked together at the California-Leidesdorff corner. It was a jerry-built shelter of scrap lumber and sheet metal and was occupied and used with the high good humor of the times. A month after the fire, the Loughborough residence at Franklin and O'Farrell streets was leased for banking premises.

There the bank remained until late in the year, when shelter at 1128 Van Ness Avenue, near Post, was completed. The Van Ness Avenue branch remained in operation two years.

On historic April 18, the day of the quake, the bank's corner at California and Sansome streets had been just a hole in the ground. But within six weeks of the earthquake and fire, the officers of the bank were authorized to get the new building under way. The site once had been the edge of the bay, and a pile-driver which was set up in the excavation sank six feet by its own weight. Piles were driven one on top of the other, three-deep. Low-bed trucks, drawn by 18-horse teams, brought the big granite columns in sections through the streets. Chain blocks lifted and placed them. By midsummer of 1908, the structure was virtually completed. The bank prepared to leave its various temporary quarters.

The transfer began at the close of business on Saturday, September 5, and continued over the weekend. Late Sunday night, securities and coin to the amount of $54,000,000 were moved down California Street from Leidesdorff to Sansome, and deposited in the new vaults. Monday was devoted to completing the transfer of records and equipment and to preparations for the opening the next morning. From 10 o'clock in the morning until long after regular banking hours, September 8, 1908, the building was thronged with visitors.

Pedestrians inspecting the cooled bricks and walls on California Street
looking east from Kearny — April 1906.

Sansome and Bush Streets. Ordinary office safes were shambles, but bank vaults largely remained intact. Chief danger to contents was an inrush of air from opening before the vaults had cooled.

President King said of the new structure, "The directors thought it their duty to put up the best bank building in the United States to show their absolute confidence and faith in San Francisco in spite of the disaster which has befallen." The erection of the massive building helped to implement the popular cry, "Don't talk earthquake, talk business!"

The big banking room, 112 feet by 80 with 60-foot ceilings, won the viewers' admiration. It is indeed one of the most beautiful in the country. The granite used in the exterior construction was mined and cut in the Sierra. A ram's head at the entrance of the building and a pair of California mountain lions over the vaults were the work of sculptor Arthur Putnam.

To many people this return of the bank to its long-time site symbolized the re-establishment of the financial district in its traditional location. During the nearly 40 years the bank had occupied the California-Sansome corner, the bank had attained a position that was in many ways unique among Pacific Coast financial houses. The *Pacific Banker*, published in Portland, said in 1907, "The Bank of California is not the largest bank in San Francisco, though it is one of the largest. It is the oldest commercial bank. . . . Faithful service has ever been rewarded whenever there was an opportunity. . . . The bank has not only evinced the good habit of holding on to its officials and rewarding its clerical force, but also of maintaining a good grip on its patrons, both in the form of borrowers and depositors. Square and courteous treatment has been the rule toward all clients. That course always brings the best returns in the end. The bank has ever sought to be helpful to the community, and to the banks as well. It has assisted in financing a good many large undertakings of a public or quasi-public character. It is one of the best-known banks on the Coast. It is also one of the widest known."

FRANK B. ANDERSON
The Bank's 5th President, played a leading part in creating the Federal Reserve System.
He served from 1909-1925.

For a score of years about the turn of the century, one of the bank's leading spirits was Charles R. Bishop, long of Hawaii. Two years before the California gold discovery, Mr. Bishop had set sail from New York for Oregon via Cape Horn. His brig touched at Honolulu. He met the Hawaiian princess Bernice Pauahi Paki, a daughter of the Kamehamehas. Plans for Oregon went glimmering. Young Bishop married the princess, went into business, became Collector of Customs for the island kingdom, served as Minister of Education, helped the island group become the most literate in the Pacific, and founded a bank, Bishop & Company—now the First National Bank of Hawaii. It has long been The Bank of California's correspondent in Hawaii. In the 1890's, a widower with a half century of solid accomplishments in the Islands, Bishop moved to San Francisco. The Bank of California elected him to its board and made him its vice president—the second (after William Alvord) to hold that office. He was a pillar until his death in 1915 in his 93rd year.

Homer S. King was the bank's president, 1904-09, serving it through the panic of 1907 when the nation's stock markets tumbled and hand-to-hand money largely disappeared from circulation. In more than 50 cities, clearing house certificates were resorted to. Under Mr. King, who was also still the San Francisco Clearing House Association's president, $12 million in this form of improvised currency was issued. For San Francisco, the fact was of especial interest: the paper, backed by good security deposited by the member banks, was accepted by the general public in lieu of gold. But it became clear to practically all bankers that a strong central bank was needed as a source of legal and more elastic currency. When Frank B. Anderson became The Bank of California's head, he played a leading part in the creation of such a nation-wide system. The Federal Reserve Act, urged by the nation's bankers, was approved December 23, 1913. The system is empowerd to supply legal currency known as federal reserve notes against good security deposited with it by its members. Mr. Anderson was a member of the organizing committee that set up its twelve districts. The Twelfth Federal Reserve District is comprised of California, Oregon, Washington, Idaho, Nevada, Utah, most of Arizona, and Hawaii and Alaska. San Francisco was made the site of the Federal Reserve Bank of this 716,000-square-mile district, and branches were opened at Portland, Seattle, Spokane and Los Angeles. C. K. McIntosh, vice president of The Bank of California, was one of "The Fed's" directors, in which capacity he served for many years.

In 1910, as the new century ended its first decade, The Bank of California made a second historic merger.

The San Francisco National Bank was the lineal descendant of Sather & Church, founded in 1850. Pedar Sather and Edward W. Church were New Yorkers who had come west with the Gold Rush. Later they took in another

The Bank of California, N.A., Head Office, 400 California Street, San Francisco, since 1908. The new structure, extending to Leidesdorff, will include this building as the main banking room.

partner, Francis M. Drexel of Philadelphia. When one of San Francisco's many early-day fires razed much of the town including Sather & Church's banking house, another was erected at the northeast corner of Montgomery and Commercial streets. This was at the end of the "Long Wharf." The manager of the bank slept on the premises and rose each morning to greet the river boats arriving from Sacramento and Stockton. His duty was to dicker with returning miners for their pokes of gold.

Only once in those turbulent times of frequent bank failures was Drexel, Sather & Church compelled to close its doors. This was in November, 1857. It was caused by financial panic then prevailing in the East, and by the sinking of the steamer *Central America*, on which the firm had shipped a large amount of treasure. Drexel, Sather & Church promptly published a statement showing

The present Head Office at 400 California Street during construction, 1907.

assets $464,000; owed to depositors, $242,000. All obligations were paid in full and the partnership bank soon resumed. In the next 40 years it operated successfully under several names, in 1897 becoming the San Francisco National Bank. The merger with The Bank of California took place sixty years almost to the month after Sather & Church first nailed its sign to the shanty on piles at the seaward end of Washington Street. In those six decades the population of the United States had increased from 23 to 92 million.

In 1910 The Bank of California, after operating 46 years under the banking laws of the States of California, Nevada, Oregon and Washington, became a national bank. The change did not involve capitalization or management. It carried with it the privilege of operating across state lines where the bank already had branches. The Bank of California, National Association, became and still is the only national bank with direct offices in three states.

While cannonading in World War I shook much of the world beyond the U. S. borders, a quiet demise took place on the other side of the Sierra Nevada. The Virginia City agency of The Bank of California, which had played such a signal part in the Comstock Lode's career, passed into history, as the bank's other Nevada offices had done at Treasure Hill, White Pine, and Gold Hill.

In 1919 the bank acquired the commercial, savings, trust and safe deposit business of Tacoma's Fidelity Trust Company, a highly respected institution organized in 1889. By the amalgamation, the Tacoma branch of The Bank of California, N.A., doubled its deposits.

Back in the year the Liberty Bell rang out for American independence, the Spanish explorer-colonist de Anza established a presidio overlooking the Golden Gate. Padres of the expedition set up a Mission a few miles south. In its heyday the "Mission Dolores" furnished employment and religious instruction for about 800 Indians. About that venerated adobe structure, the Mission District of San Francisco later evolved. It developed a distinct personality and contributed much to the growth and prosperity of the city.

When population and business activity warranted a bank in 1903, Mission Bank was established in the district. In all the area between downtown San Francisco and the city of San Mateo 16 miles down the Peninsula, it was the first and for a time the only commercial bank. (The region today contains about 50 banking offices.) The Bank of California was Mission Bank's majority stockholder.

Mission Bank's first president, James Rolph, Jr., became a nationally-known figure as San Francisco's mayor and California's governor. He was the son of James Rolph, The Bank of California's long-time head note teller. The bank became the Mission Branch of The Bank of California in 1927.

CHARLES K. McINTOSH

Under President C. K. McIntosh from 1925, the Bank ably withstood the stresses of the depression. To the various governmental measures taken to relieve the situation, it lent loyal support. At the same time, it was unyielding in its opposition to inflationary measures and to other proposals inconsistent with the principles of sound banking.

JAMES J. HUNTER

In 1938, James J. Hunter became the 7th president and Charles K. McIntosh chairman, until the latter's death in 1948. Hunter served until January 1, 1950. The Bank was rounding out its first three-quarters of a century.

The gold scales in the Auburn office. Still in use, they have weighed millions of dollars in Placer County gold.

The Changing Economy

Through much of the nineteenth century, a national goal had been the transfer of seemingly limitless government lands into the hands of individuals or groups who could utilize them. This had been undertaken through various homesteading acts, timber-cutting acts, and huge land grants to railroads, schools and colleges. In spite of many abuses, the measures had brought about land distribution and settlement. By the century's end, a frontier line no longer existed. Westward settlement had become a filling-in process.

Railroads and the refrigerator car had helped to bring about a striking change of scene. West Coast wheat lands, the crops of which had gone chiefly to Europe, were being cut up into diversified farms and orchards. Irrigation was increasing. Mechanical power was assisting and then replacing animal and human power on the farm. With better seed, fertilizer and scientific methods, less man-power on the land was producing greater crops.

Industry was striding with seven-league boots. The census of 1890 was the first to report the nation's manufactures' value greater than agriculture's. By 1900 it was twice as great. The United States was becoming the world's leading industrial nation.

Golden Gate Bridge — gateway to the Pacific. San Francisco is shown in the background.

73

The movement to the cities was a notable social change. And cities were taking on a new look. In the two decades before and after the turn of the century, electric trolley lines had made suburbs possible. Out of labor-management conflicts and adjustments came higher wages, shorter hours, more time for the expanding interests of each individual. Installment buying was on the increase. Mass consumption was pacing mass production. In 1900, the automobile was a curiosity. In 1910, a hundred thousand cars were produced. In 1917, two million.

The years just preceding the first World War are now looked back upon as perhaps the most tranquil the world has ever known. Europe had been at peace for two generations. Armed hosts drilled in many countries, but for those who watched them march by they were merely parts of a colorful pageant. Chancelleries wrote notes of professional politeness to each other. War was beginning to be considered obsolete. Science was international. Trade was good. The major diseases were being conquered. Taxes were low. The United States had no federal income tax. "Trusts" were being "busted," but a man lucky enough to make a lot of money could keep all of it.

The Liberty Loan campaigns of World War I taught large numbers of people to invest their savings in government bonds. From bonds they turned to the stock market. In addition, the great public utilities had taught employees and consumers to invest in their preferred and common stocks. The industries of the country were going more and more into the hands of the people of small wealth. From investment to reckless speculation proved but a step.

Looking back on 1927, Chairman Frank B. Anderson advised The Bank of California stockholders at their annual meeting: "Speculation, aided by cheap money, has run riot throughout the country. . . . a very large percentage of our population has been tempted to buy stocks on margin. . . . The lessons of the past are shown but scant respect and we are told that we must adjust ourselves to modern methods and conditions, but it is our opinion that what are today called old fashioned methods, will have more respect paid to them five years from now than they have today."

The crash came. Before the disaster was stemmed, the United States had 12 million unemployed, the nations of the world were off the gold standard and world trade was down 70 percent.

Among the changes wrought by the depression upon the Pacific Coast was the disappearance of gold money, and its replacement by paper currency. When the government called in all gold and locked it into vaults at Fort Knox, the eight-decade rule of King Gold and Queen Silver on the Coast came to an end. Another western custom also had been disappearing—the aversion to pennies. Once all settlements, even at the banks, had been made to the nearest nickel. The rise of street car fares from 5 cents to 6 had made copper pennies essential. Sales taxes also rushed the trend along. The great Mint at Fifth and Mission streets in San Francisco, which had coined over $103 million in gold in one year before the Fire, and never a copper penny until 1908, at last turned energetically to the task of making one-cent pieces. The West's high, wide contempt for the humble brown coins, as for paper currency, had gone the way of Steamer Day and the clipper ships.

The 1930's had seen suffering and anxiety. They also had seen the erection of Boulder, Shasta, Bonneville and Grand Coulee dams, revolutionizing the heavy construction business and western power and irrigation. The decade had seen the erection of the world's longest over-all bridge and the world's longest single span bridge, over San Francisco Bay and the Golden Gate. Nuclear discoveries were being made in Dr. Lawrence's Cyclotron at Berkeley. The atomic age was already being envisioned by a few men.

Social and economic changes launched by the depression were profound. A reliance upon government aid for the individual became a growing habit. Taxes rose, the national debt rose. The purchasing value of the dollar fell. Inflation created a host of new problems.

National defense production, and suddenly World War II, came to the nation. And with them, expansion into industry such as the West Coast had not known before.

In Southern California, shipbuilding and plane building challenged or exceeded all records being established anywhere. About San Francisco Bay, industrial cities sprang up overnight in marshlands and hayfields. Oakland imported entire trains from New York's defunct Sixth Avenue El to carry shipbuilding commuters to Richmond. In Nevada, whistle stops and sagebrush flats became storage and distributing centers for enormous dumps of ammunition and other supplies. Tacoma found itself the hub of three major military installations. Between '41 and '45, a large ocean-going vessel of some type went down the launching ways in Portland's vicinity at an average of one each 24 hours. Seattle's Boeing works became one of the nation's great war arsenals. From Tucson to Bellingham and Boise to San Diego, hammers rang and welding arcs flared.

The rising cost of government was enormously speeded by World War II and it has since become commonplace for peacetime costs to maintain that galloping increase. Public welfare outlays alone by federal, state and municipal governments doubled between 1955 and 1963, totaling more than $40 billions. The $3,207,000,000 California state budget for fiscal 1964 exceeded by $100 million the entire federal budget of 1928.*

America realized that to do more and pay for more, it must produce more.

---

*Newsweek, June 24, 1963.

From Ox Team to Airplane

WITHIN the span of his adult life, Ezra Meeker, pioneer and trail maker, has witnessed the development of transportation from the ox team to the airplane.

It has been permitted him to cross the continent in turn by covered wagon, railway train, motor car and "flying machine"—a gamut of experience embracing practically the entire lifetime of the Pacific Coast.

About the time he turned his cattle Westward, some sixty years ago, The Bank of California was founded. It, too, has lived through this great formative period and had a part in "the making of the West."

Today it has four offices, Seattle, Tacoma, Portland and San Francisco, a national association with resources of more than $100,000,000. Its 60 years experience serves many new-comers in the West.

The BANK OF CALIFORNIA N.A.
(A NATIONAL BANK)
815 Second Avenue   Seattle

GODFREY L. WAKEMAN   HERBERT V. ALWARD
JOINT MANAGERS
LEON F. MACKLEM, Asst. Manager   ROBERT B. SNOWDON, Asst. Manager
JOSEPH C. GLASS, Asst. Manager   WALTER A. HEATH, Asst. Manager

Bank advertisement on the 60th anniversary

The incredible output of the country lifted the gross national product to new heights year by year and actually resulted in the amazing spectacle of a nation having far more food than it knew what to do with. Farmers were being paid by their government to produce less of several basic crops. No nation ever before faced such a surprising problem.

Meanwhile, the United States contributed its share to the worldwide "population explosion," In the Pacific states, growth was augmented by migration from other sections at an accelerated pace. It became, in a sense, an explosion riding on a landslide. A generation before, there had been "dust bowl" migrations, to escape disastrous drouths in other parts of the country. Then came extreme "pie in the sky" programs or trends in some of the western states. In most cases the newcomers remained to become sturdy, independent, hardworking citizens. They, and those who followed to work in the defense plants, found desirable climates on the West Coast; greater recreation facilities; economic opportunity. Many of the arrivals were simply responding to the "Go West, young man" impulse that has led men and families over rivers and plains and mountains Pacific Coastward for a hundred years. The very words California, Oregon, Washington, have glamour. And the distances hither have shrunk. People come no longer by ox wagon in months. They come in days or in hours by car, bus, train and plane. It was "the second discovery of the West."

Fortunately an industrial base had been laid to support greatly increased population. The shipyards had been temporary, but the airplane plants had come to stay. The Coast at last produced steel. It produced aluminum, and had the electric power to do it. In the Columbia basin, Bonneville and Grand Coulee dams had been only starters. Upward of thirty dams on the Columbia and its tributaries were under construction or being planned. Petroleum and natural gas would soon begin arriving from Alberta by way of British Columbia. A multi-billion dollar water project was launched for California. Missile and electronic industries unimagined in magnitude were in the near future. Los Angeles, that city of unstoppable growth and energy, was advancing to third in size in the nation and California was soon to be the most populous state.

But the unexpected retention of the "temporary" migration raised housing problems all over the Coast. War housing had been temporary and much of it had to go. New roofs had to be raised for the occupants. The return of veterans from the armed services, many of them intent on founding families, added to the housing shortage. There was widespread discomfort and a frenzied building boom aided by federal loans. Housing developments pushed out into fields and orchards and over rolling hills. Express highways were rushed from the older urban centers. Bumper-to-bumper traffic moved where lately only a country lane wandered.

The movement was chain-reacting. As newcomers wrote home of the opportunities on the Coast, succeeding waves of people poured in, eager to share in the rediscovered western frontier. Building enough schools, finding teachers, developing water systems and extending the utilities became critical matters. And still the houses clambered up the hills and spilled through the gaps.

Population of the three Pacific Coast states, 9,733,000 in 1940, by 1960 had topped 20 million. Some 11.4 percent of the U. S. population was in these three states. The gain is still surging on, with forecasts of a three-state population of 29,000,000 in 1975.

The Bank's Main Office in Modesto.
The founders of the City of Modesto wished to name it "Ralston,"
but his modesty caused them to name it "Modesto."

The Crossroads

For the first ninety of its one hundred years, The Bank of California had grown steadily if not spectacularly. With a single brief exception, its four score years and ten had been an unbroken success story, punctuated to be sure by crises of varying intensity, but always moving ahead with assurance and dignity. By the beginning of 1954 its capital funds had multiplied 13½ times, rising to more than $27 million from the original $2 million put up by Messrs. Mills, Ralston and their associates. Its deposits had reached nearly $400 million, loans were above $170 million, and total resources exceeded $440 million.

Viewed in the abstract, these were accomplishments to be proud of, and the clients of the bank took perhaps greater pride in them than did the bank itself. Many of them were leaders in the West's civic, cultural and commercial affairs, descendants of families and businesses whose fortunes The Bank of California had helped to found in the early days. For them, this was "their bank"; substantial, solid, unchanging.

But in the west of the postwar 50's nothing was unchanging. Change was the order of the day, and the forces of growth—in population, industry, hous-

One of the many extensive freeway systems that make an easy entrance to San Francisco.

ing, distribution—drove relentlessly for expansion or extinction. Retailers who had prospered with big city stores found their markets decentralizing, and established suburban branches to follow their business. Manufacturers found the new west too big and promising to serve from their eastern plants, so created full-fledged manufacturing and assembly plants in the west. Increasingly efficient transportation and communication encouraged people and industries to move out from the cities, and shopping centers sprang up to serve them at home.

In the general atmosphere of change, the banking industry was going through a revolution of its own. As early as the 30's, some banks in the west had begun to "popularize" banking, introducing consumer banking services, embracing the burgeoning business of consumer credit, placing small neighborhood branches in the new communities that began even then to develop. In these efforts they were aided by a benevolent government which encouraged consumer spending and consumer lending, fortified by a war-born production capacity which in the late 40's turned its strength to consumer goods and created new markets, emboldened by an inflationary cycle of higher wages and purchasing power. All of this came to focus in California where the booming population exaggerated and accelerated an economy that was expanding in all parts of the country.

The result was a new 20th century bonanza for the branch banking systems, and in California, Oregon and Washington they flourished with unparalleled vigor. In the older, small communities independent banks, which had grown quietly with their constituencies, yielded to the flattering offers of the branch systems and joined them. In the fresh new suburbs and raw young towns, the big banks established new offices which grew with the communities they helped to develop.

As often happens in the saga of successful institutions, The Bank of California had men to match the challenge. In 1950, Elliott McAllister became the eighth president of the bank, and along with him into management came Edwin E. Adams as executive vice president. Of vastly different backgrounds, they combined the blue blood of tradition with the red blood of ambition to create a management team remarkably suited to the critical needs of the time. McAllister, a native San Franciscan and a graduate of the University of California, was head of the bank's Foreign Department before his election to the presidency. Adams had come up through the ranks in the Seattle office and advanced to the management of that office before being called to San Francisco as the second in command.

With its five major offices in all three west coast states, The Bank of California was a most attractive prize for banks with merger on their minds. In the early 50's several overtures were made, but it was not till the summer of 1954 that the moment of real decision came. The prospect of a three-way merger, in which The Bank of California would join with another traditional northern

ELLIOTT McALLISTER

The Bank's 8th President, McAllister established the important doctrine of expansion which began
in 1954. Through the ensuing 9 years he served as Chief Executive Officer (President 1950-1956,
Chairman of the Board 1956-1963) and brought The Bank of California from a 5-office complex to
a billion dollar 35-office, tri-state system. He continues to serve the Bank as a member
of the Board of Directors and its Executive Committee.

California bank and a major system based in Los Angeles to form the nation's only coastwide bank, led the bank's board of directors to a deep self-appraisal of its position and its future. From this critical consideration came a confident, courageous, concise statement of policy:

"We are convinced that with our fine old name and the loyalty we enjoy from clients and shareholders alike, we should do everything possible to develop and strengthen the bank as an independent institution, substantially unchanged in character.

"It is our plan to add additional branches, both through the acquisition of existing banks and the starting of new offices in areas determined to be favorable for our operation. . . .

"At the same time we will proceed to develop to the maximum extent the activities of the present branches in Portland, Oregon and Seattle and Tacoma, Washington . . ."

With this pronouncement the old era of five-major-office banking, which had existed unchanged for nearly 50 years, ended and the era of expansion began. Within the next ten years, the bank would more than double in every measure of size and strength, and before its 100th birthday would join the select company of billion dollar banks.

The decision to expand was speedily converted to action with the addition of the first new office in August, 1954. This was the 81-year-old Bank of Martinez, acquired by merger.

In the following year The Bank of Berkeley was merged and new offices were opened in Oakland, and in Burlingame-Millbrae on land which years before had been the home of the bank's first president, D. O. Mills.

Seven offices were added in 1957, three in California's Central Valley with the merger of Modesto Bank and Trust Company, one in the East Bay with the acquisition of The First National Bank in San Leandro, one in Auburn by merger with Placer County Bank, and new offices in Santa Rosa to the north and San Jose to the south.

The following year, except for the opening of the bank's Palo Alto office (home of Stanford University), was given over to a period of digestion. In three short years the bank had grown from 5 to 17 offices and had entered a whole new field of retail banking in new communities where the high concentrations of newcomers to California were not so aware of its age and tradition. As the bank expanded its physical plant, it was also necessary to expand internally in personnel and in breadth of new services. Integration of the growing system required the development of new departmental structures, establishment of policies to cover countless details, and the careful selection and training of officers for future branches. In every way the bank was expanding its scope: its client base broadened and diversified, its service base widened and varied.

These changes took time and, most importantly, the kind of care which would preserve the bank's traditional quality of personal service as it reached more and more people.

In 1959, the pace of expansion resumed, proceeding along a carefully planned course. The "master plan" was difficult to see in the first few years, with new offices being opened in widely separated communities. But by January of 1962, when it published a review of expansion progress in the 1961 Annual Report, the pattern was clear. The original decision to expand was implemented by two additional decisions: (1) to concentrate in California while maintaining its major offices in the northwest; and (2) to establish a grid of key offices in major northern California cities, supplementing them with satellite offices in the communities surrounding these major cities.

EDWIN E. ADAMS
9th President of The Bank of California, 1956-1962;
Vice Chairman of the Board, 1962-1963;
Chairman of the Board, 1963.

By early 1962, in its 98th year, the bank's system had grown to 30 offices, its capital funds exceeded $50 million and its total resources were well above the $800 million mark. In that year, the bank took another significant step, as far-reaching in its way as was the declaration of expansion in 1954.

On June 1, 1962, the Board of Directors elected a non-banker as President, succeeding Mr. Adams who had become President in 1956 when Mr. McAllister became Chairman of the Board. Charles de Bretteville, at age 49, was the young president of Spreckels Sugar Company. He had been a director of the bank for 10 years and was intimately familiar with its operations through his service

Marble-sheathed 12-story building at 550 South Flower Street, Los Angeles, acquired by The Bank of California to house its Southern California Headquarters, opened in August 1963.

on almost every Board committee. By education, Stanford and Harvard School of Business, he was eminently qualified to assume a major administrative role. By experience, he had proved his capacity for leadership. And by heritage, he was intimately associated with the west and its traditions.

He was not an armchair executive. Within a few weeks, no branch manager was surprised to see him striding in the door; no department head nor staff member had reason to wonder who he was. He moved throughout the bank's marketing area, meeting customers and employees, talking business, talking banking, taking action. He traveled the east, the midwest, the south and southwest, and he concluded that The Bank of California had the greatest franchise in American banking—with one exception.

In November, 1962, the bank announced that approval had been requested from the Comptroller of the Currency for the establishment of a major southern California headquarters in downtown Los Angeles. In February, 1963, the bank purchased the 12-story Superior Oil Company Building at Sixth and Flower Streets. The lower floors were speedily transformed into luxurious banking quarters, the name was changed to Bank of California Building, and on August 16 was opened for business.

With this single, but signally important, addition The Bank of California became a truly coastwide institution, capable of serving the entire banking needs of any client throughout the entire Pacific Coast. And around the Los Angeles nucleus, it is expected that additional branches will be added. At this writing, June, 1964, a merger with the 8-office American National Bank of San Bernardino has just been completed, raising to 45 the total number of offices.

In mid-1963, plans were also announced for the construction of a new 20-story Head Office Building in San Francisco, to be erected on California Street adjacent to the present building. By early 1964, various banking departments had been removed from the old Annex and were re-distributed throughout 10 buildings within a few blocks of 400 California Street. It is expected that this dispersion will be reversed sometime in 1966, and all administrative offices of the bank re-established then in the new building.

Another planned major building project is the construction of a new building for the Portland office where a full city block has been purchased. Plans and studies are currently underway with prospects for construction to start in the near future.

Internally, the bank's organization has been strengthened by the advancement of several key officers to the rank of senior vice president, two to executive vice president, and the addition of a number of outstanding executives. Most encouraging for the future has been an infusion of bright, ambitious young executives from all parts of the country who see in The Bank of California a fast-moving rapidly developing organization with great opportunity for them.

Mr. Adams became Chairman of the Board on the retirement of Mr. Mc-

CHARLES DE BRETTEVILLE
Became the Bank's 10th President in June, 1962, and assumed the duties of Chief Executive Officer
upon Elliott McAllister's retirement in late 1963.

Allister late in 1963, and did himself retire at the end of that year. Together they had guided the bank through one of its most decisive periods; together they had helped make possible the kind of institution which in 1964 has become known as "the bank for action."

The writing of history depends in large part on perspective, and it is difficult to analyze current events with assurance, even more hazardous to try to forecast the future. Yet some observations may be made.

A fundamental element in the expansion policy announced by the bank in 1954 was that it should remain "substantially unchanged in character." If ever an institution had a clearly defined character it was The Bank of California in 1954. Sometimes referred to affectionately as "The Old Lady of California Street," the bank was then known and respected as old, honorable, rich, and conservative—a banker's bank. Its fame had spread to the far corners of the earth, and among professionals it occupied a position of great distinction. Its clients took almost proprietary pride in claiming The Bank of California as their own, and nearly resented the relative newcomers who could not look back on so long a relationship. But admirable as it was, it was a bank whose glories were in the past.

No one can think of The Bank of California in those terms today. With aggressive determination, a clean competitive resolve, and an organization geared for action, The Bank of California has added a rising spirit of youth and vigor to its mantle of tradition. Today it provides every banking service for every need, large and small. Its Head Office at 400 California Street is still a national symbol of the grandeur of banking; yet it is intimately related to a pleasantly informal and rustic banking office in a peninsula town, to a granite structure nestled between modern skyscrapers in Seattle, and to a tiny bank which occupies one of Monterey's oldest Spanish haciendas. The bank's visitors in a single day may include the chief executive of a multi-million-dollar corporation and a young man financing a car. The Corinthian columned facade of its San Francisco headquarters is as classically beautiful as ever, yet it no longer awes a public which has come to know that this bank is warm, friendly, professional and personal—that it has not forgotten that each individual's financial business is of surpassing importance to him—that however large or small one's affairs may be, this is a good bank to grow with.

The Bank of California is fortunate indeed to be located in the center of the nation's most dynamic area. Every index, every forecast points toward continued growth for the west coast in the years ahead. With its own expanding structure and its boundless confidence, there is every reason to believe The Bank of California will share in this growth in full measure.